GW00545205

RAF Jaguars provided sterling service in the Gulf War of 1991, operating from Muharraq, Bahrain, from where they generated 617 combat sorties. Performance was considerably better than anticipated. Four Royal Ordnance 1,000-pounders, as seen here, made up a typical mission load, as were the unconventional overwing AIM-9L Sidewinder AAM configuration and the outboard Westinghouse AN/ALQ-101(V)-10 ECM and slimmer Phimat chaff pods. (Royal Air Force)

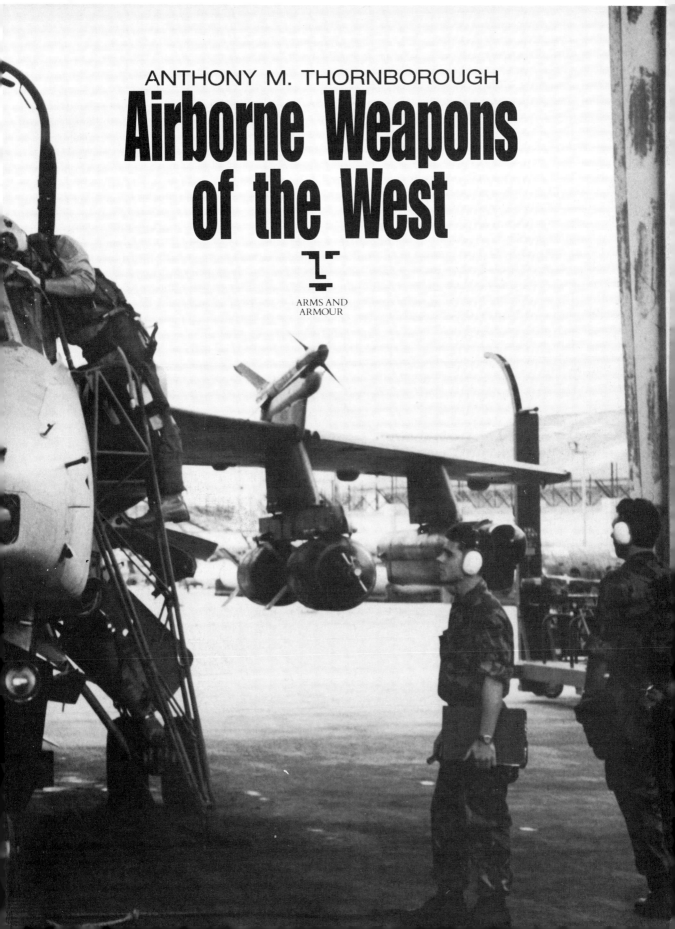

ANTHONY M. THORNBOROUGH

Airborne Weapons
of the West

ARMS AND
ARMOUR

Arms and Armour Press
A Cassell Imprint
Villiers House, 41–47 Strand, London WC2N 5JE.

Distributed in Australia by Capricorn Link (Australia) Pty.
Ltd, P.O. Box 665, Lane Cove, New South Wales 2066.

British Library Cataloguing-in-Publication Data: a
catalogue record for this book is available from the
British Library

ISBN 1-85409-119-0

Edited and designed by Roger Chesneau.
Typeset by Wyvern Typesetting Ltd, Bristol.
Camerawork by M&E Reproductions, North Fambridge,
Essex.
Printed and bound in Great Britain by The Bath Press,
Avon.

CONTENTS

INTRODUCTION

During the course of the lightning six-week 'Desert Storm' air war over the Persian Gulf the world was presented with the evidence of the destructive power of modern airborne weapons systems: videotaped electro-optic imagery from the targeting devices carried by American, British and French fighter-bombers was broadcast on television news bulletins around the world as mute, eerie testimony to the devastating surgical bombing available to Coalition commanders. Although many of these devices saw their genesis two decades ago, the world's media lavished their mixed praise on the 'new' weapons, which came into their own over Baghdad. Nobody can possibly forget the harrowing images of the crosshaired targets erupting in plumes of smoke. At bomb release slant-ranges of three miles, these were struck with an accuracy measured in inches! Backstage, while the 'smart' attackers dropped bridges, put penetrating bombs down the ventilator shafts of bunkers and 'plinked' individual tanks with the apparent macabre ease of a teenage arcade game, bombers deposited everything from Korean-vintage 'dumb' bombs and rockets to napalm and propaganda leaflets. Within a few days the Iraqi military infrastructure had been cut off at the neck and its beleaguered troops shocked into capitulation. Not since the 'Little Boy' and 'Fat Man' nuclear attacks by 'Enola Gay' and 'Bock's Car' on Japan in August 1945, or the Arab-Israeli 'Six Day War' of 1967 when the Cheyl Ha'Avir successfully demolished the opposition on the ground in a pre-emptive strike, have airborne weapons proved to be so decisive. The concept of 'victory through air power', espoused by the aviation pioneers Giulio Douhet and Billy Mitchell and the Second World War hard-liners 'Bomber' Harris and Curtis LeMay, was realized once again. Perhaps

more significantly, as General Merrill A. McPeak, USAF Chief of Staff, noted, 'Desert Storm' represented 'the first time in history that a field army has been defeated by air power'.

This book examines the weapons systems that made the Allied forces so effective in the Persian Gulf—the bombs, missiles and targeting aids that are the tools of their trade—together with those that did not, and the reasons why, some of them political in nature. Also covered is the broader gamut of offensive and defensive weaponry that equips the air arsenals of Western Europe and the United States, while attention has also been focused on some of the latest developments. 'Desert Storm' successfully exorcised the Vietnam ghost. Nonetheless, the United States and its allies are well aware that they must not rest too heavily on their recent success: the next adversary may be much, much better prepared, and weapons systems take time and a great deal of money to evolve. Newer, more autonomous, even 'smarter' devices are currently in development and are competing for funds in the present austere defence world. So, while the actual employment of airborne weapons during recent conflicts forms the core of this book, the work is also intended as a general review of today's leading-edge airborne armaments—including nuclear bombs and missiles, which have successfully kept the peace for over forty years. The latter are now in a welcome state of decline in line with the perceived threat—a simple case of 'mission accomplished', now that the 'Bear' is similarly clipping its claws—though there will exist a need for retaliatory devices of mass destruction until the world is rid of the unconscionable despots into whose hands the technology is falling.

A small section of this book has also been

devoted to some of the more esoteric 'strap-ons' which are regularly seen bolted to front-line combat aircraft—not weapons *per se*, but electronic warfare devices and targeting pods—and which form an integral part of every top-of-the-mark fighter-bomber's 'kit', permitting it to penetrate hostile defences relatively unmolested and to deposit muni-tions on target with pinpoint accuracy. These are more than just a mere adjunct to the weaponry: they are one of the keys to their success. As a result, the author makes no apology for concentrating on the technology used by the US, British and French services, as these are the most prominent, in both sen-ses of the word. The only caveat is that readers expecting a lengthy dissertation on guns and rockets should examine other sources devoted to close-ups of breeches and steel tubes. The inherent simplicity of such devices combined with their use nowadays only in low-threat areas or aboard comparatively primitive aircraft precludes detailed discussion here. However, where credit is due they have been mentioned. Certainly, the powder-pushed projectiles are as lethal to 'that frail pink thing' (as one com-bat pilot described himself) as is the most sophisticated missile; perhaps for those very reasons the subject is more suited to a book on *anti-air*! It is hoped that by skirting around that now much discussed area of airborne weapons, now firmly superseded by missiles and PGM technology, readers are permitted to examine in greater detail the more nail-biting hardware.

Finally, in line with the thinking of the fight-ing men in the air, the book draws on such widely used euphemisms as 'taking out' (born in Vietnam) and 'plinking' (one of those to emerge from the Gulf War, based on teenage 'gopher shoots' in the backwoods of the US), when one really means killing. While air crews always claim to 'go for the machine', few of their targets are inanimate. It is hoped that these expressions do not cause offence. Certainly, the author has not lost sight of the dreadful things these destructive devices do to people, whatever the morality of the cause. In this context it is worth reiterating an oft-repeated phrase: 'That we possess such weapons often prevents far worse evils'. Sadly, civilization remains a terribly fragile thing.

A number of people gave their time freely in order to supply copious notes, drawings, photos and constructive thoughts for use in this book—some based on direct combat or engineering experience, some more dialectic in approach (and some a combination of the two, relative to the degree of beer con-sumed!)—and the author is sincerely indebted to them all for their considerable generosity: Col. Walter Berg, USAF; August H. Bichel; Kearney Bothwell; C. Bushey; Roger Chesneau; Peter E. Davies; David M. Dodds; Dale Donovan; R. Thomas Duncan; Norma L. Gibson; Haydn L. Hughes; Ian Hun-ter; Mike Holloway; Fg. Off. N. R. Jones, RAAF; Mike Keep; Tim Laming; Tim Lewis; Lois Lovisolo; Frank B. Mormillo; Tim Perry; David Robinson; Maj. Jim Rotramel, USAF; Bettie E. Sprigg; Lt. Col. Jim Uken, USAF; Vincent Vinci; James S. Wilson; Lee Wooley; and the numerous air crews not mentioned above but from whom the author snatched a few enlightening quotes during trips to air bases and delightful displays. Mention should be made of the organizations behind several of these names, including: Brunswick Defense; Dassault-Breguet Aviation; the US Department of Defense; the Australian Departments of Defence; GEC-Marconi; General Electric (USA); Grumman Archives; Hughes Missiles; IPMS-UK; Israeli Aircraft Industries; Linewrights; Lockheed ASC; Pinpoint Models/PP Aeroparts; RAF Strike Command; Reheat Models; Raytheon Miss-iles; Rockwell International; the US Navy; and the US Air Force. Thanks are also due to Rod Dymott, Director of Arms & Armour Press, for backing the project to begin with, and to the design and production teams—Roger Chesneau of Linewrights in particular, who may have paced the floor awaiting the final draft!—who transformed the typescript and stack of support items into this book. My sincere thanks to you all.

Anthony M. Thornborough
Bristol, December 1991

1.
FOX ONE, TWO, THREE

AERIAL COMBAT has been the ultimate test of the mettle of men since the heady and dangerous days of 'The Great War', when such types as Camels and Fokkers exchanged machine-gun fire in classic, swirling dogfights, snatching bites out of each other. Today, seventy-five years later, the psychology remains the same but the technology involved would be nothing short of mind-boggling to those aviators of yesteryear. Costing £20 million apiece, made of metal, crewed by one or two fighter 'jocks' cocooned in an environmentally controlled cockpit, and each weighing up to twenty-five tons, modern fighters get into the fray in stages, as befits their complexity. Engagements with the opponent start with beyond visual range (BVR) radar lock-ons at a distance of up to 150 miles, followed by a 'Fox One' shot, with radar-homing air-to-air missiles (AAM) let loose before even the enemy's canopy or leading edges, let alone his flying goggles, glisten in the attacker's vision. As range closes to within the minimum of the stand-off 'BVR kill box', the next volley comprises 'Fox Two' or 'Heater', using infra red-homing missiles honed to pick up the passive electromagnetic radiation emitted by the quarry's engines, its aerodynamically warmed airframe and its volatile fuel tanks. As the deadly confrontation between the 'knights' develops into a mêlée at close quarters—known to all as the 'Fur Ball' or 'Knife Fight'—the gun comes into play, yet even this comparatively simple device bears little relation to its forebears. A truer analogy (etymologically at least, *missile* owes its origins to the language of the Ancient Mediterranean) would be with the Phalanx of the Greek Hoplites, which in formation threw javelins, lobbed shot and then drew swords, strictly in that order. Whatever the origins of this new orthodoxy, the presence of the AAM

was ushered in by the collision-course missile—the javelin of the 1950s.

The first to appear was the far-from-sleek Douglas AIR-2A, a tubby white missile boosted by a Thiokol TU-289 solid-propellant rocket which delivered 36,000lb of thrust to provide a burn-out speed of Mach 3.3 and a range of six miles—all very impressive but actually terribly crude. It was introduced as a stop-gap measure under Project 'Ding-Dong' pending the introduction of the finesse

◀ In its element: an F-15A air superiority fighter of the 43rd TFS based at Elmendorf, Alaska (and currently assigned to Pacific Command), soars skyward near Mount McKinley brandishing a full complement of live AIM-7F Sparrow III and AIM-9L Sidewinder AAMs. Arctic patrols are taxing, but pilots are given almost unparalleled freedom to 'turn and burn' noisily. (McAir)

inherent in guided missiles, and as such used sledgehammer tactics: using only stabilizing 'pop-out' fins and a gyro to steady it as it plied its ballistic track, and proximity fuses to set off its W25 1.5-kiloton TNT-equivalent nuclear warhead, the aptly named Genie 'puffed' into a 1,000ft fireball. As a Montana Air National Guardsman described it, 'The Genie was one of those great misconceived ideas of the "Fabulous Fifties" which reasoned that a large air-to-air missile equipped with a "nuke" [warhead] would be just the ideal thing for breaking up Russian bomber formations as they battled their way south from the Pole. Apparenty, little thought was given to the "friendlies" underneath the flight path and what Genie would do to them!' In fact, on 19 July 1957, when the threat of the Soviet bomber was reaching paranoid proportions, a live weapon was shot above the Continental United States (CONUS) from an F-98J Scorpion, as a display of this new defensive force—though in this instance over the unpopulated wasteground of Yucca Flat, Nevada, where it would do no harm! Production of the missile ended in 1962 yet the weapon remained the 'last resort' AAM of the North American Continental Air Defence forces (NORAD) throughout the 1960s and 1970s on board F-101B 'One-O-Wonders' and the F-106A 'Sixes' of Air Defense Command (ADC), until eventually withdrawn from the inventory, along with the last vestiges of the 'Six', during 1987.[1]

Supplementing Genie on board all these

peaceful giants was the Hughes Falcon, the world's first true guided AAM. The pet project of the eccentric billionaire Howard Hughes, the Falcon achieved Initial Operating Capability (IOC) with the F-89D Scorpions of NORAD's ADC during 1955, and it represented an enormous step forward. So advanced was it (on paper, at least) that it was initially classed as a *fighter aircraft* and styled the XF-98! Initiated in 1947 as the Tiamat, by 1962 Project 'Dragonfly' had evolved through several GAR designations to become the AIM-4 Falcon 'family'.[2]

Built in two key production formats by Hughes at Culver City, California—the Mach 3-capable double-cruciform Falcon, and the Mach 4-capable extended-chord Super Falcon—it came with one of two types of guidance: semi-active radar homing (SARH), whereby the weapon homes in on an aerial target 'painted' by the launch aircraft's fire control radar; and inert, nitrogen-cooled, heat-seeking infra-red, whereby, at closer quarters, the missile would be cued to target using a combination of the launch aircraft's radar and an infra-red search and track sensor (IRSTS). Like the Genie, the Falcon enjoyed production as a W25-toting nuclear weapon (the AIM-26A), alongside a comparatively innocuous counterpart which packed a 40lb conventional warhead (the 'Bravo' equivalent). It has now been retired from the USAF inventory, and from those of its customers, Canada, Sweden and Switzerland. Production continued up to 1963 and eventually totalled some 60,000 rounds, with updates lasting for a further six years, while its tried-and-trusted design went on, in scaled-up fashion, to form the basis of many of today's best guided missiles, including the Maverick and the Phoenix.[3] Falcon was also a weapon which truly 'kept the peace'. Only the AIM-4D-for-dogfighting model ever saw combat, aboard Phantoms of the USAF and Israeli *Cheyl Ha'Avir*. It achieved mixed results because of its contact fusing, which required a direct hit every time, and because of its reliance on an IRSTS for initial target acquisition, making it better suited to the big 'Century Series' interceptors keeping intruders at bay from the North American Continent. Nonetheless, it accounted for some seven MiGs before it was withdrawn in favour of the world-class Sidewinder.[4]

Impressed by the sensible philosophy embodied in Falcon of producing one basic

◀ The Hughes GAR-1, AIM-4A Falcon (front) was one of the most sophisticated AAMs in the world when it achieved IOC in 1956. It metamorphosed into the long-finned AIM-9E/F/G series, then into the nuclear-capable AIM-26A, and ultimately into the GAR-9, AIM-47A Super Falcon (at rear). Although incredibly complex and prone to numerous teething troubles, the 'family' sired today's AIM-54 Phoenix, the world's longest-ranged AAM. (Hughes)

▶ The Montana ANG based at Great Falls were one of the last units to fly the F-106A/B Delta Dart—known to all as the 'Six'. Departing alongside the glossy grey jets in 1987 were the last remaining AIM-4F/G Falcon and Genie AIR-2A missiles. The captive blue, finless ATM-4 round protruding from the Delta Dart's weapons bay was called a WESM (Weapon Evaluation System Missile) which, at the crucial moment of 'launch', would pop-out of the bay to photograph the target. (Mil-Slides)

THE FALCON FAMILY

Model designations			Seeker	Principal aircraft user	Related control system	Range (miles)
Old DoD	**Hughes**	**USAF**				
GAR-1	DPa	AIM-4 Falcon	⎱ SARH	F-89H Scorpion	E-9	⎱
GAR-1D	DPb	AIM-4A Falcon		F-101B Voodoo	MG-13	6
GAR-2	FPa	AIM-4B Falcon	⎱ IR	F-102A Delta Dagger	MG-10	⎰
GAR-2A	FPb	AIM-4C Falcon				
GAR-2B	FPc	AIM-4D Falcon	IR	As above, plus F-4D, F-4E/EJ	APQ-109 APQ-120	6
GAR-3	EPa	AIM-4E Super Falcon	⎱ SARH			
GAR-3A	EPb	AIM-4F Super Falcon		F-106A/B Delta Dart	MA-1	7
GAR-4A	GPb	AIM-4G Super Falcon	IR			
GAR-11	52	AIM-26A Nuclear Super Falcon	⎱ SARH	F-101B, F-102A		5
GAR-11A	52A	AIM-26B Super Falcon				
GAR-9	50	AIM-47A Super Falcon	Active/data-link	F-108 proposal, YF-12A	ASG-18	115
XAAM-N-11*	92	AIM-54A Phoenix	Active/data-link	F-111B, F-14A	AWG-9	130

*US Navy designation
Notes: The name Falcon was adopted on 8 February 1950. The B was a transitionary model to the C. The Swedish J35F Draken used the Saab SARH R327 (AIM-26B) and IR R328 (AIM-4C); the Swiss Mirage IIIS used the HM55S (R327-cum-AIM-26B). A nuclear version of the AIM-47 was in development before project termination.

airframe with two different forms of guidance honed to the talents of domestically manufactured fighters, in 1957 France's SA Matra company embarked on the R530 project to equip the nation's fledgeling Mirage III. The SARH model, equipped with the EMD AD26 seeker, was introduced in the early 1960s, matched to the best-selling Mirage's Cyrano radar—and later the APQ-94 of the *Aéronavale*'s F-8E(FN) Crusaders—along with a heat-seeking model fitted with a SAT AD3501 nose. Performance—a maximum range of 11 miles and a burn-out speed of Mach 2.7—fell far short of that of the Ameri-can AAMs, yet it sold well as part of numerous Mirage-related joint deals and laid the groundwork for the much-improved Super 530 of the 1970s and today's *Missile Intermédiare de Combat Aérien*, the MICA.[5]

DESERT RATTLERS

While the USAF battled with sophisticated Hughes radar, IRSTS and Falcon missile 'packages' linked to NORAD's Semi-Automatic Ground Environment control (SAGE, which in its all-up configuration permitted 'hands off' target vectoring and automatic weapons launch), the US Navy opted for a

different approach, in keeping with the simpler, less sophisticated jets embarked on board its carriers.

Developed by China Lake's Naval Ordnance Test Station in California, Sidewinder actually began life as the 'garage' creation of NOTS engineer William B. McLean, a nervous genius from the 'mad professor' mould. He scrounged parts from various sources, including the NOTS scrapheap, and designed 85 per cent of the missile in his spare time. Sidewinder comprised a simple aluminium tube fitted with a small charge, a rocket motor and a heat-detecting cell. Simplicity was the key: the prototype had a total of nine moving parts and its 'brain' a mere seven radio tubes! Known to the engineers involved as Local Project 612, it was still a back-room experiment with no official funding when the first successful test shot was achieved on 11 September 1953 in the skilled hands of Walter 'Wally' Schirra. Not to be

upstaged, the Air Force requested a fly-off with the Falcon missile, while US Navy personnel, now developing a keen interest in Sidewinder, stood back and stayed *very* quiet. An elderly F-86 carrying one of McLean's jury-rigged LP612 Sidewinders went up and casually knocked down its assigned target drone with one shot. 'For six straight days the Hughes team struggled with the Falcon and their tons of test and support equipment', according to McLean's assistant Howard A. Wilcox, but their beloved protégé refused to leave the launcher, too nervous to take the plunge. Then, out of desperation, the US Air Force ordered another Sidewinder shot, and another drone was destroyed. Adding insult to injury, the unassuming McLean asked if he too could have some *test* equipment: he needed a step-ladder and a torch to assist with checking-out another Sidewinder, before it too successfully 'zapped' its drone! Wilcox later recalled that the

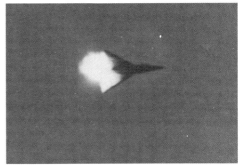

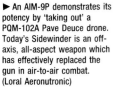
Falcon 'was so damned complicated and expensive that they couldn't fire it unless it was perfect. Our philosophy was, when the pilot hits the "pickle", the missile goes'. McLean received a plaque from President Eisenhower and a bonus cheque for his efforts. The rest is history. Sidewinder remains the world's most effective point-and-shoot AAM thirty years later, in use with over two dozen nations. Its operation remains simple: selected and pointed physically in the direction of the target, the pilot waits for a low-pitched 'growl' (or the newer versions' 'chirp') to come on the headset, telling him the missile has acquired it, and then presses the firing trigger. Longer-ranged results are achieved by using preliminary vectors from the fighter's radar and inertial navigation set. Once launched, the 'Winder goes about its business unaided.

Manufacture of the missile began with the fine-tuned AIM-9B production version which was subcontracted to Philco Ford and General Electric and achieved IOC with the US Navy in May 1956. This philosophy of farming out production to various sources remains in use and has consistently kept prices down. Some fourteen US companies, led by Loral Aeronutronic (formerly Ford Aerospace) and Raytheon, compete to make its various parts, while vying with one another to bolster technology. Updates have gradually expanded the capability of Sidewinder,

reducing the solar 'dead zone' and opening up the missile's launch envelope from the early shoot-into-the-tail 'Bravo', through the Sidewinder Expanded Acquisition Mode (SEAM) 'Golf' of 1967, effective in the rear and flank quadrants, to the modern off-axis, all-aspect 'Lima' and 'Mike' versions, which began to roll off the production lines in the mid-1970s (see accompanying table). The US Navy and Air Force also, for a while, adopted two quite different approaches: on the heels of the 'Bravo' the Navy switched to the 'Delta', which introduced gas refrigeration to enhance seeker sensitivity, whereas the Air Force opted for Peltier-effect thermoelectric cooling on its new 'Echo'. The Navy approach currently is the vogue, using argon or nitrogen gas cooling.[6]

Today's superlative AIM-9L was blooded in the Gulf of Sidra in August 1981, when a pair of VF-41 *Black Aces* Tomcats from the USS *Nimitz* returned fire on a pair of Atoll-

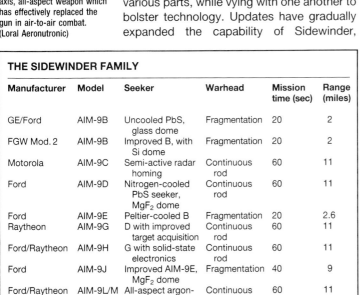

THE SIDEWINDER FAMILY

Manufacturer	Model	Seeker	Warhead	Mission time (sec)	Range (miles)
GE/Ford	AIM-9B	Uncooled PbS, glass dome	Fragmentation	20	2
FGW Mod. 2	AIM-9B	Improved B, with Si dome	Fragmentation	20	2
Motorola	AIM-9C	Semi-active radar homing	Continuous rod	60	11
Ford	AIM-9D	Nitrogen-cooled PbS seeker, MgF_2 dome	Continuous rod	60	11
Ford	AIM-9E	Peltier-cooled B	Fragmentation	20	2.6
Raytheon	AIM-9G	D with improved target acquisition	Continuous rod	60	11
Ford/Raytheon	AIM-9H	G with solid-state electronics	Continuous rod	60	11
Ford	AIM-9J	Improved AIM-9E, MgF_2 dome	Fragmentation	40	9
Ford/Raytheon	AIM-9L/M	All-aspect argon-cooled InSb seeker	Continuous rod	60	11
Ford	AIM-9N/P*	J with active optical fuse	Fragmentation	40	9

*AIM-9J-1 became the -9P in 1978. The -9N is the FMS export model. Active optical fusing is fitted to the AIM-9P-1/3 variants only.

armed Libyan Sukhoi 'Fitters'. A further 25 'kills' were chalked up in the South Atlantic the following spring when Royal Navy Sea Harriers took on Argentine Mirages and Skyhawks; Britain owes a great deal to the 100 'Limas' supplied on the orders of Navy Secretary John F. Lehman, without strings. The AIM-9L, and the United States' exclusive 'Mike' follow-on, remain the primary short-ranged armament of most Western fighters. The Sidewinder is also being built under licence in Europe by Bodensee Geratetechnik of Germany and Saab of Sweden, while America is in turn starting up production of the AIM-9R, developed as a sideline to Project 'Pave Prism'. This last version employs an imaging infra-red seeker in lieu of the traditional gas-cooled seeker, for reduced complexity backed with faster lock-on. Including updates, production of all marks of the AIM-9 has surpassed 100,000 rounds.

Snake names are the norm for the heat-loving slender weapons, so when Israel embarked on its own offshoots of Sidewinder it too classified its derivatives under the genus *Orphidia*. In an effort to ensure a steady supply of AAMs through the ups and downs of international embargoes, the fledgeling nation took the American AIM-9B Sidewinder, made it yet simpler by fine-tuning it to the less exacting, local clear-weather climate and created the Shafrir 2. This entered service in time for the great dogfights fought over the Sinai during the War of Attri-

◄ The pale grey AIM-9L/M in detail. The weapon features advanced cryogenic cooling and microchip electronics and gets its target in over 90 per cent of launches. The original AIM-9A version, known during its inception in 1953 as Local Project 612, was the brainchild of China Lake engineer William McLean. The pod to the left is an Air Combat Maneuvering Instrumented (ACMI) transmitter, which relays aircraft movements and actions to the ground-based Cubic Corporation ACMI and TACTS (Tactical Air Combat Training System) range computers. (Raytheon)

◄ Clad in cumbersome NBC (nuclear, biological and chemical) protective suits, a trio of ground crewmen load a live AIM-9L on to a Phantom FGR.2 during exercises at RAF Wattisham. The red-tagged safety pins and yellow 'noddy' caps protecting the seekers are removed immediately before aircraft take-off during the Quick Reaction Alert scramble. (Royal Air Force)

◄ This fine study of an F-16B at Nellis TFWC, Nevada, shows off the ACMI training pod and outboard Sidewinder launch rails to good effect. (Raytheon)

► A slinky grey F-14A Tomcat of VF-102 *Diamondbacks* sporting massive air-to-air punch, including live AIM-9M Sidewinders and AIM-7M Sparrows, fuel tanks, a 20mm M61A1 'Gat' gun fairing and a nose-mounted Northrop TCS (Television Camera System) which is used positively to identify radar bogeys at BVR. Tomcats from VF-41 *Black Aces* were the first to employ the all-aspect Sidewinder in combat: on 19 August 1981 'Fast Eagle 107', flown by Lts. Larry Muczynski and James Anderson, and 'Fast Eagle 102', crewed by Cdr. Henry Kleeman and his NFO Lt. Dave Venlet, each 'splashed' a Libyan Su-22 'Fitter' over the Gulf of Sidra. (Raytheon)

▲ The shape of the future: the Lockheed/Boeing/General Dynamics F-22 Advanced Tactical Fighter beat the Northrop/McDonnell Douglas YF-23 submission during a competitive 'Dem Val' conducted at Edwards AFB, California, during 1990. The aircraft is a through-and-through 'fourth-generation' stealth design and carries its Sidewinder and AMRAAM missiles internally. (Eric Schulzinger/Lockheed)

sequently downed received mortal wounds from the Python 3. Owing to its swept fins and more dynamic shape, this indigenous development ostensibly shares very little with its forebears. Yet it is a direct descendant, employing the same slipstream-driven stabilizing tailfin 'rollerons' introduced by the Sidewinder, along with similar guidance and propulsion systems. Its short-range performance is claimed to be on par with that of the AIM-9L. Covert exchanges of data are doubtless in progress.

Equally successful is Matra's Mach 3 R550 Magic, the standard weapon for *Armée de l'Air* fighters 'on heat' and for numerous overseas clients which since 1982 have included fourteen nations dotted around South America, Southern Europe and the Middle East. Interchangeable with Sidewinder and its back-up nitrogen cryogenics, the R550 began its development in 1968 and IOC with the Magic 1 was achieved seven years later. It is, however, an all-new weapon with a triple set of cruciform canards reminiscent of modern AAMs of Soviet origin, and it has proved its ability to engage targets at ranges down to 300m (330yd) and to pull 50*g* in snap manoeuvres to catch its prey—a force which would break any aircraft up into pieces and turn its pilot into jelly. The all-aspect Magic 2 of the mid-1980s introduced a Richard butylane high-impulse solid rocket motor, an all-aspect seeker capability and the ability to be cued to target via the launch aircraft's fire

tion in 1970, where it claimed a success rate of 65–70 per cent—marginally superior to America's then top-of-the-line SEAM AIM-9G. A bigger cylinder (1.3in wider than the AIM-9 series) enabled its manufacturers Rafael to squeeze in more propellant and a larger, 4kg (8.82lb) proximity- and impact-fused blast-fragmentation charge. Successors followed. Twelve years later, in June 1982, when *Cheyl Ha'Avir* fighters wheeled aggressively over the Lebanon, many of the 85 Syrian 'Fishbeds' and 'Floggers' they sub-

◄ Some of the ordnance available to the multi-role Mirage 2000, including 68mm rockets, 30mm cannon, R550 Magic 2 and R530D Super AAMs, ATLIS laser marking pod and ancillary 'smart' bombs and missiles, along with Exocet, Durandal and Belouga munitions. (Dassault Aviaplans)

◄ France has 'gone it alone' to develop the superb Matra R550 Magic 2 and Super R530D air-to-air missiles, tailor-made for the Mirage 'family'. The Magic 2 is installationally interchangeable with the American Sidewinder. These two photographs show slick Mirage 2000C-RDIs, from *5ᵉ Escadron de Chasse* based at Orange, toting two of each missile along with a centreline 1,300-litre capacity fuel tank. This unit was deployed for combat in the Gulf and achieved an operational readiness rate approaching 100 per cent. (SIRPA Air)

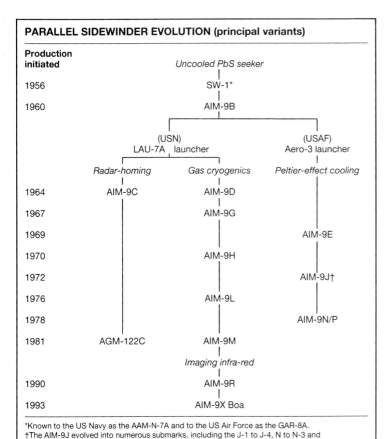

PARALLEL SIDEWINDER EVOLUTION (principal variants)

Production initiated			
		Uncooled PbS seeker	
		SW-1*	
1956			
		AIM-9B	
1960			
	(USN) LAU-7A launcher		(USAF) Aero-3 launcher
	Radar-homing	*Gas cryogenics*	*Peltier-effect cooling*
1964	AIM-9C	AIM-9D	
1967		AIM-9G	
1969			AIM-9E
1970		AIM-9H	
1972			AIM-9J†
1976		AIM-9L	
1978			AIM-9N/P
1981	AGM-122C	AIM-9M	
		Imaging infra-red	
1990		AIM-9R	
1993		AIM-9X Boa	

*Known to the US Navy as the AAM-N-7A and to the US Air Force as the GAR-8A.
†The AIM-9J evolved into numerous submarks, including the J-1 to J-4, N to N-3 and subsequently the P to P-3 series, all fundamentally similar but employing improved fusing and other minor refinements.

Enter its intended successor, the Advanced Short-Range AAM (ASRAAM), which was thrown open to competition once more following a decade of relatively stagnant development. America and Europe are now treading separate paths, though the philosophies remain the same: by employing modern digital autopilot electronics it has become possible to ditch draggy superfluous aerofoils—the traditional forward steering canards and chunky rollerons—in favour of aerodynamically refined control surfaces which will improve speed and range. Moreover, manoeuvrability is enhanced by several orders of magnitude by taking advantage of the weapon's natural instability (kept in check for most of the flight), enabling it to zoom away at higher angles of attack in bank-to-turn fashion by 'toppling' into the desired new heading as required. Other features common to the ASRAAM/SRAAM competitors include a multi-element heat-seeking 'eye', along with a low-smoke engine and reduced radar signature to defeat modern missile approach warning systems (MAWS)—devices which will soon be linked to laser guns to destroy the AAM's delicate homing electronics. The latest USAF contender is the Raytheon tail-controlled adaptation of the AIM-9M, the test firings of which commenced over the steamy Eglin Munitions Systems Division (MSD) range in 1990, to score five 'kills' in eight launches—a fantastic start given the inevitable teething problems encountered with new weapons. The NWC, in collaboration with General Dynamics, has similarly tested a trimmed-down 'Mike'. This also 'scored' during its first outing, on 25 September 1990. Both developments will likely coalesce to satisfy the joint service requirement for the AIM-9X SRAAM, the

control radar—a method adopted by the Sidewinder in lieu of IRSTS when Phantoms began trading in their radome-mounted AN/AAQ-4 infra-red sensors in favour of radar-warning receivers.

The future of Sidewinder remains in limbo, the basic technology having reached a development plateau beyond which further improvements are difficult to implement.

► Edwards' test force is currently engaged in trials over nearby China Lake of the new Raytheon advanced infra-red-guided, tail-controlled missile—an offshoot of the Sidewinder AIM-9M/R. America is pursuing two such concepts to fill the gap created when it left the European ASRAAM programme. (Raytheon)

under Project 'Hot Shot'. This 'rode' a radar beam pointed at the target from the launch fighter by means of passive dipole antennae built into the skin of the missile, and was effective up to a range of around 5 miles. Some 2,000 examples of this AIM-7A model were built, and it entered limited operational service with the US Navy's Skyknight, Cutlass and Demon fighters during July 1956.

Concurrent development by Douglas and Bendix Pacific produced the Sparrow II (AAM-N-3 and AIM-7B), an active radar-equipped missile responsible for 'painting' its own target, which had an effective range of only about 1 mile. A little background theory explains why this AAM was so ambitious. As Raytheon put it when looking at the limitations of the Sparrow II active system, 'Only a very small fraction of this power reaches the target and is reflected, and an even smaller fraction [10^{16} times smaller] of that is intercepted by the missile antenna as a signal. Electronic circuits try to detect this signal and recognize it as coming from the desired target. This problem has been likened to that of trying to hear a pin drop a mile away while yelling at the top of your lungs.' The technology simply was not available thirty years ago to make this concept work. Sparrow II never entered operational service, and both early birds were soon ousted by Raytheon's far superior AIM-7C Sparrow III. This was assured of success because of its precision-engineered SARH guidance system tailored to work with the powerful Westinghouse APG-51A radar, packed into the pioneering Demon, on which the system achieved IOC in 1958. As Raytheon had realized, SARH permitted the key transmitter and receiver to be isolated from one another: the big radars tucked behind the matt black fibreglass radomes of the Demon, and later the Phantom, did the 'yelling', while the SARH Sparrow III headed out and picked up the weak echoes from the 'painted' target, using a gyro-stabilized, gimballed seeker which moved to compensate for missile pitching manoeuvres. It was a staggering piece of engineering for its day, and the product of much blood, sweat and tears: early pilot production rounds typically required a month of 16-hour-long days to check-out prior to flight, even after passing the best factory test procedures that could be devised.

Entering pilot production in 1956, the AIM-

◄ The RAF's principal interceptor of the 1960s and 1970s was the Lightning, which carried a modest quantity of heat-seeking AAMs: two each of either the white Firestreak or the follow-on metallic-coloured Red Top. The Red Top strapped to the flank of this F.6 features dark green fins. (C. F. E. Smedley)

◄ BAe Dynamics are busy at work on the AIM-132A Advanced Short-Range AAM (ASRAAM), one of several new-generation agile missiles which employ rear-steering 'flippers'. This pair are depicted in their would-be operational configuration on the Tornado F.3. (BAe Dynamics)

definitive 'Sidewinder' (to be christened the Boa, in keeping with China Lake's codename for their creation). On the other side of the Atlantic, work on the maturing Anglo-German AGM-132A ASRAAM continues, drawing on Germany's expertise gleaned during Sidewinder update programmes and Britain's once progressive efforts which ended two decades ago with the successful conclusion of the 'Red Top' programme. The eventual winner has yet to be decided, and when it does the primary contractors can expect total revenues to be worth billions.

SPARROW

Another famous missile 'family' which owes its origins to the endeavours of the US Navy in the early 1950s is the widely used AIM-7 Sparrow, developed for use on the Service's F3H Demons, and subsequently the F-4 Phantom—which latter was conceived originally as a mere Sparrow *platform*. The weapon began life as the ambitious XAAM-N-2 Sparrow I in 1946, developed by Sperry

► The AIM-7C Sparrow III achieved IOC with the F3H Demons of the US Navy during 1958. This photograph was taken during 1956–57, during the pilot production phase, when the Point Mugu, California-based Pacific Missile Test Center conducted operational trials with the radical new weapon. Later aircraft adopted a conformal mode of weapons carriage. (Raytheon)

▼ Zoom! An AIM-7E-2 Sparrow III heads for its radar-painted quarry during 'William Tell 84'. The launch aircraft was an F-4D 'Rhino' assigned to the North Dakota ANG at Fargo, which flew under the tradename *The Happy Hooligans*. (Capt. Larry Harrington, North Dakota ANG)

7C was superseded four years later by the 'Delta' with a revised liquid propelled motor, in turn replaced by the solid rocket motor of the 'Echo' in 1963. Featuring a 66lb warhead, a burnout speed of Mach 4 and a range of up to 30 miles when launched at altitude, all these missiles had but one function: carried semi-recessed in quartets on the broad belly of the F-4Bs of the US Navy/Marines and the F-4Cs of the USAF, they were designed to intercept large, relatively unmanoeuvrable 'Badger' and 'Bison' bombers, which would typically be engaged with radar using BVR techniques: the Phantom's radar was locked on to the target by the guy-in-the-backseat at a range of up to 40 miles, and the pilot in turn was provided with a steering dot and angular error circle on his miniature radar repeater scope which enabled him to position the jet on an optimum intercept course for a missile attack. Fine though this was for the Fleet Barrier Combat Air Patrol (BARCAP) and Continental air defence missions, it soon proved inadequate for 'dogfighting', where the fast-

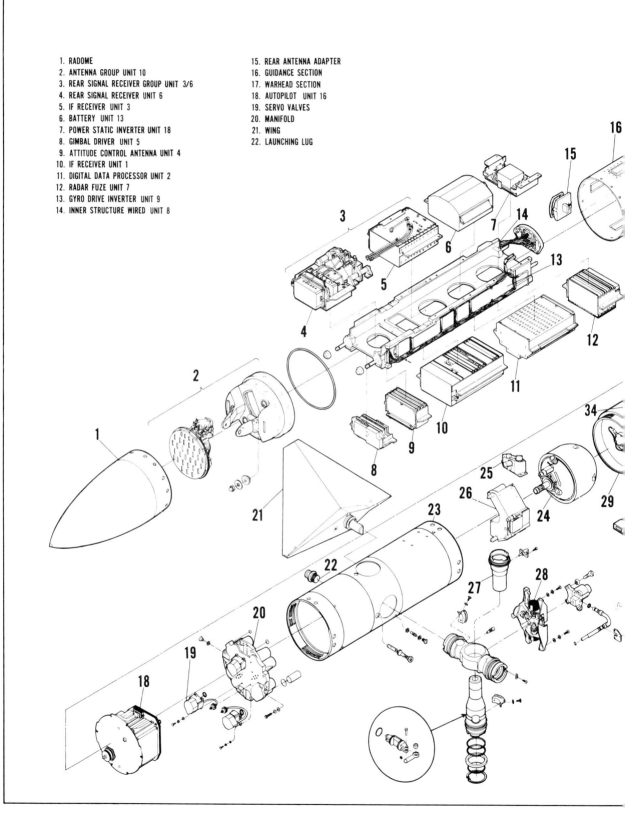

1. RADOME
2. ANTENNA GROUP UNIT 10
3. REAR SIGNAL RECEIVER GROUP UNIT 3/6
4. REAR SIGNAL RECEIVER UNIT 6
5. IF RECEIVER UNIT 3
6. BATTERY UNIT 13
7. POWER STATIC INVERTER UNIT 18
8. GIMBAL DRIVER UNIT 5
9. ATTITUDE CONTROL ANTENNA UNIT 4
10. IF RECEIVER UNIT 1
11. DIGITAL DATA PROCESSOR UNIT 2
12. RADAR FUZE UNIT 7
13. GYRO DRIVE INVERTER UNIT 9
14. INNER STRUCTURE WIRED UNIT 8

15. REAR ANTENNA ADAPTER
16. GUIDANCE SECTION
17. WARHEAD SECTION
18. AUTOPILOT UNIT 16
19. SERVO VALVES
20. MANIFOLD
21. WING
22. LAUNCHING LUG

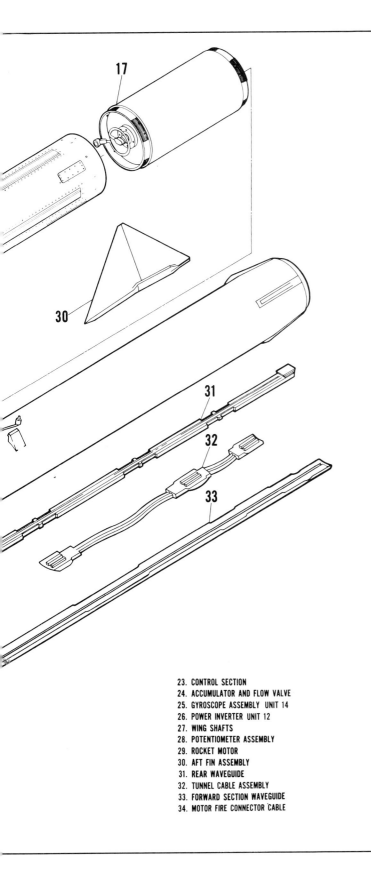

23. CONTROL SECTION
24. ACCUMULATOR AND FLOW VALVE
25. GYROSCOPE ASSEMBLY UNIT 14
26. POWER INVERTER UNIT 12
27. WING SHAFTS
28. POTENTIOMETER ASSEMBLY
29. ROCKET MOTOR
30. AFT FIN ASSEMBLY
31. REAR WAVEGUIDE
32. TUNNEL CABLE ASSEMBLY
33. FORWARD SECTION WAVEGUIDE
34. MOTOR FIRE CONNECTOR CABLE

paced, turning-and-burning nature of the battle at close quarters often precluded a satisfactory radar lock: in such scenarios, peering out of the cockpit was a necessary measure to prevent the hunter from becoming the hunted!

Another key issue was reliability. Engineer Mike Fossier has described the situation from Raytheon's perspective: 'When Sparrow was designed it was envisaged that the missile would be loaded only in time of war and fired at bomber aircraft approaching the Fleet. The critical period of reliability was therefore thought to be the half-minute of missile flight, to which it would be subjected shortly after fighter take-off. In Vietnam, these conditions did not apply. The North Vietnamese did not use air power to attack the Fleet or other US positions; instead, they used interceptors at isolated times and under conditions of their choosing to try to disrupt US air raids. As a result, months would go by without air combat. During these months, the Sparrows would be carried daily in a fully operating state on F-4s conducting ground attack missions of several hours each'. Naturally enough, the crews expected the weapons to work on an 'as-required' basis, despite the daily rigours to which the Sparrows were being subjected. What resulted was performance akin to a 'lucky dip': Sparrows sometimes glided to target under austere conditions at the edge of their theoretical envelope; at other times they went 'ape', even when fired within perfect operating parameters. The kill probability (pK) rates were in the order of 10 per cent.

The first ever Sparrow 'kills' were achieved during the opening clashes of the 'Rolling Thunder' campaign against North Vietnam. On 17 June 1965 a pair of VF-21 *Freelancers* F-4Bs from the USS *Midway*, skilfully flown by Cdr. Louis Page and Lt. Cdr. John Carl Smith Jr., and Lt. Jack Ernest David Batson and Lt. Cdr. Robert Bartsch Doremus, downed a pair of MiG-17s with AIM-7Ds. However, this sort of action grew ever more scarce as the doctrine of the war deteriorated into gradualism. The air-to-air Rules of Engagement (ROE) grew steadily more strict, stipulating positive visual identification. This followed a couple of 'own goals', one of which witnessed a Sparrow acquire a 'lock' on an Australian motorboat (which presented

◄ Component breakdown of the Raytheon AIM-7M Sparrow III SARH missile. (Raytheon)

SPARROW EVOLUTION

Manufacturer	Model	Guidance	Production initiated	Range (miles)	Remarks
Sperry	AIM-7A	Radar beam-riding	1951	5	Sparrow I. Manufacturer's designation AAM-N-2. Limited production.
Bendix	AIM-7B	Active radar-homing	1951	10	Sparrow II. Manufacturer's designation AAM-N-3. Limited production.
Raytheon	AIM-7C	SARH	1955	25	Sparrow III. Manufacturer's designation AAM-N-6. IOC 1958.
Raytheon	AIM-7D	SARH	1959	25	Enhanced reliability. IOC 1960.
Raytheon	AIM-7E	SARH	1962	28	Solid rocket motor. IOC 1963.
Raytheon	AIM-7E2	SARH	1969	28	Dogfight capability. IOC 1970.
Raytheon	AIM-7F	SARH	1974	62	Extended range. IOC 1975.
BAe	Sky Flash	SARH	1976	31	Manufacturer's designation XJ521. Reduced warm-up time, monopulse seeker. IOC 1978.
Selenia	Aspide 1/1A	SARH	1978	62	Extended performance. IOC 1979.
Raytheon	AIM-7M	SARH	1980	62	Combines best of AIM-7F and Sky Flash. IOC 1983.
Raytheon	AIM-7P	SARH	Current	62	Pre-programmable.
Raytheon	AIM-7R	SARH	Under development	–	Secondary IR seeker.

a perfect radar 'blip' against the backdrop of the sea) and the other a friendly fighter-bomber shoot-down, owing to unreliable IFF (identification friend or foe) transponders and the technical limitations of the missile. As a result of the then understandable ROE, many Sparrows were fired much too close to their dynamic prey: the 3g-limited AIM-7C–E series was unable to 'snap' around in the more energetic manner required for close-quarters combat, and very soon came to play second fiddle to the Phantoms' back-up Sidewinders and hastily-installed 20mm gunpods.[8] Throughout much of the latter half of the 1960s it was the cannon-equipped F-8 Crusader which held the crown as the US Navy's 'MiG-Master'.

Thus was born the AIM-7E-2, developed by a Raytheon team led by Paul Travers, offering double the manoeuvrability and 'snap-shoot' potential. Entering pilot production in 1968 and employed in combat *en masse* during the big Vietnam 'Linebacker' aerial offensives of 1972 and Arab-Israeli clashes of October 1973, it gained fame as the legendary AAM of the era and placed the F-4 Phantom back in the limelight as supreme 'MiG-killer'. Five American and an undisclosed number of Israeli 'Fox Four' Aces owe much to the AIM-7E-2. They not only enjoyed a genuine radar-guided 'dogfight' missile for the first time in the history of aerial combat, but also were able to get maximum use out of the later-model Phantoms' auto-acquisition avionics, which caged

the fire control system at boresight for visual radar lock-ons—tactics espoused by the newly formed F-4 Top Gun and Fighter Weapons schools, which aimed to combine the best of technology with sharp flying skills. This profound philosophical change, from intercept to dogfight missile, concentrated

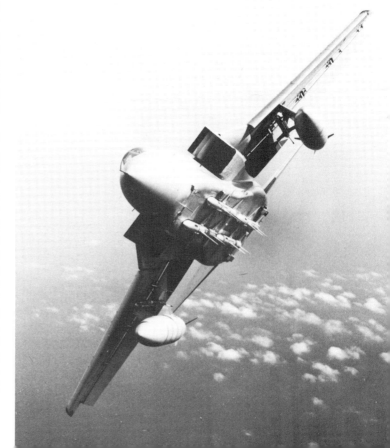

► The 4485th Operational Test Squadron, its headquarters Gen. John Corder's USAFTAWC at Eglin AFB in Florida, is the key unit responsible for ensuring that Combat Command's sizeable fighter community is kept up to date with the latest Sparrow, Sidewinder and AMRAAM developments. The AIM-7M model soaring away from this F-15A features an inert warhead. (Raytheon)

Sparrow's minimum-range performance too.[9]

By 1974, Raytheon had switched to more resilient, solid-state electronics to produce the AIM-7F, which employed traditional continuous-wave SARH guidance matched to the digitally updated 'super search' capabilities of LRU-1-Mod F-4E Phantoms, as well as to the new range of Doppler radars and acquisition modes available to the awesome F-14 and F-15 twin-engined 'Teenagers'. Above all else, the 'Foxtrot' featured an improved 88lb fragmentation warhead shifted into the missile's forebody, facilitated by the miniaturization of the guidance electronics. This in turn permitted Raytheon to turn the entire rear section of the weapon over to propulsion, thereby doubling maximum range to a staggering sixty miles—yet minimum range was improved once again such that it overlapped that of guns, permitting the missile to be sequenced into rapid play should the need arise. Five years later production shifted to the microchip AIM-7M, which achieved IOC during 1983. This offers yet greater reliability and counter-countermeasures, claim the manufacturers. Prior to 'Desert Storm', pilots flying the big 'Teenagers' claimed that they were able to set up an impenetrable BVR 'kill box' extending from an altitude of 150ft to the stratosphere. Computer-monitored mock air combat exercises held at the American instrumented combat ranges backed up their claims, though may have been based on optimistic

data gleaned from test shots made under 'laboratory' conditions. Nevertheless, the still much-maligned Sparrow lived up to most expectations during combat in the Arabian Peninsula and accounted for the bulk of the 'kills' during Operation 'Desert Storm'. The Eagle units were particularly well satisfied with Sparrow's performance, which accounted for the majority of the thirteen 'kills' scored by Bitburg's 36th TFW, the fifteen which were made by Eglin's 33rd TFW *Gulf Eagles* and the solitary 'Flogger' downed by a *Hound* from the 32nd TFG. Their coalition colleagues added to the success when Capt. Ayedh Al Shawaa of No. 13 Sqn. RSAF bagged a pair of Mirage F1EQs outbound with a lethal load of Exocets—the second 'double kill' of the conflict—also with Sparrows, conducted under the guidance of E-3 AWACS. However, the missile's reliability, described by one officer as 'spotty', cost a few lost 'kills'. The remaining successes were all achieved with point-and-shoot Sidewinders.

The latest in the Sparrow series, the US Navy's AIM-7P 'Papa', is designed to be more effective against cruise missiles, incorporating a new reprogrammable computer to process mid-course target update information relayed over data-link—now standard procedure for the radar-guided AAMs. It rightly deserves the title Sparrow IV, but for Raytheon's objections!

BAe Dynamics (formerly part of Hawker Siddeley) has taken an active interest in the Raytheon Sparrow programme ever since

◄ The RAF's mainstay air defence fighter is the Panavia Tornado F.3, equipped with Sky Flash radar-guided AAMs, heat-seeking AIM-9L Sidewinders and a pair of Mauser 27mm 'shooters'. (BAe)

◄ A Tornado F.3 on the prowl with a quartet of BAe XJ521 Sky Flash, plus four AIM-9L Sidewinders. Sky Flash entered service with the RAF during 1978 and is today the main armament of the Tornado. (Royal Air Force)

Britain became the first overseas customer for the missile, bought as part of the McAir FG.1/FGR.2 package by the Wilson Government in 1966. BAe took the AIM-7E-2, gutted it, and fitted a Marconi XJ521 monopulse SARH seeker which offered a target discrimination performance comparable to that of the AIM-7M when working against targets shielded by ground clutter, radar glint and countermeasures—but five years ahead of the American round. Moreover, it introduced faster, 2-second warm-up times compared to the irritating 15 seconds necessary to activate a -7E-2. Named Sky Flash, the first of 1,400 missiles entered service in 1978 and the weapon now forms the main armament of the RAF's sizeable Tornado F.3 establish-

ment. Exports include the R71 to Sweden for use on the JA37 Viggen, which is upgrading the weapon to R71A standard with an improved motor and guidance system. Similar work is underway in the United Kingdom. BAe's private venture Sky Flash 90 is aimed at re-equipping the missile with a Thomson-CSF active terminal seeker and Royal Ordnance Hoopoe rocket, along with a redesigned afterbody and thinner aerofoils for greater speed and range. However, the status of this go-it-alone venture has been shaky ever since the Ministry of Defence lost interest in a follow-on version in 1981, opting instead for new American missiles.

Italy, also, has used the AIM-7E-2 as a springboard for a domestically manufactured

▼ The Mirage 2000C, with Thomson RDM radar, entered service with L'Armée de l'Air during 1983 and was followed three years later by the superior C-RDI (*Radar Doppler et Impulsions*), tuned to work with the R530D SARH missile. The first to equip with the new interceptor was *2e Escadron de Chasse* based at Dijon-Longvic. (*Armée de l'Air*)

▲ The fire-and-forget AIM-120 AMRAAM, nicknamed 'Fido', goes about its business. Its active seeker requires only minimal preliminary target data courtesy of the launch aircraft's radar, hence its recent application to the diminutive, mainly clear-weather F-16 'Electric Jet'—though note the radar pod slung under this aircraft from the Eglin-based Munitions Systems Division. (Hughes Missiles)

create the 'Romeo'—the ultimate version—to supplement SARH as a hedge against heavy RF-spectrum countermeasures which might otherwise foil the radar seeker during the closing stages of the 'kill'. Applied to Soviet SA-6 surface-to-air missiles (SAMs) for two decades, modern electronics microminiaturization has permitted the comparatively tiny AAMs to employ this dual-mode approach in the one round. It takes the Falcon and R530 philosophy one stage further, and may reap benefits in terms of a reduced minimum range capability—the bane of the Sparrow during aerial combat in South-East Asia, as related earlier.

FIDO

One of the commonest complaints to be voiced by fighter pilots is the necessity continually to 'paint' the quarry with radar for the SARH missiles, right up to impact: such often serves to bring the attacker within lethal range of his opponent's short-range heat-seeking missiles and guns, while also tending to 'advertise' the fighter's position, in turn creating the demand for complex mutual support. The AIM-7R goes some way towards addressing this by permitting the attacker to disengage earlier in the combat; but even better would be what has been described as a 'Go Get Him Fido!' missile.

The requirements for 'Fido' were laid down during the exhaustive ACEVAL/AIMVAL (Air Combat Evaluation/Air Intercept Missile Evaluation) tests flown at Nellis Tactical Fighter Weapons Center, Nevada, during 1976–77. Eagles and Tomcats tangling with nimble F-5Es equipped with only 'Heat' and guns scored badly when range closed and the ensuing 'Fur Ball' stripped them of their BVR 'kill' advantage. What the big fighters needed was a missile which would combine a number of new features: fire-and-forget guidance capable of tracking targets pulling in excess of 9g amidst extensive countermeasures in a multiple-shot, multiple-target launch, and a low-smoke motor which would provide rapid acceleration to Mach 4-plus, all combined with moderate cost and high reliability.

Five manufacturers vied for the development contract and in February 1979 the list was whittled down to two: Raytheon of Massachusetts and Hughes Missiles of California. By the end of 1981, Hughes' tail-steered 'flipper' design had been selected as

and improved version, the Aspide 1. This is functionally similar to the AIM-7F, with a maximum range of 62 miles, based again on a gutted Raytheon Sparrow airframe re-equipped with a Selenia monopulse SARH seeker and a SNIA-Viscosa solid-propellant rocket. It entered service with F-104S Star-fighters of the *Aeronautica Militaire Italiane* in 1979 and has since evolved into the Aspide 1A.

With a huge stock of missiles to hand, the American Sparrow III continues to be progressively updated. Most recently, Raytheon and General Dynamics have pooled resources in a joint venture which trades as the Iriss Company. The goal is to develop an infra-red seeker for the US Navy AIM-7P to

◄ The winning, fighting-fit combination of agility and 'supercruise' P&WA YF119 vectoring engines embodied in the second YF-22A Prototype Air Vehicle (PAV) was made all the more convincing when, on 20 December 1990, test pilot Tom Morgenfield launched an AMRAAM. The missile is ejected well clear of the aircraft's weapons bay prior to rocket ignition, hence the distinctive 'puff' of smoke under the aircraft's tail. (Lockheed)

the winner, and the company was authorized to manufacture 94 test rounds, with options for a further 924 and a hint that production orders would probably tally 24,320 (17,000 for the USAF, since reduced to 15,450 in line with current force reductions, and the balance for the US Navy/Marines). Raytheon would later re-emerge as a second-source supplier, to inject some degree of competition. The resultant AIM-120A AMRAAM is a leap ahead of Sparrow. As soon as a radar 'bogey' is identified as such (by means of IFF or information relayed from a distant AWACS command post), the attacking pilot feeds the target's relative bearing and velocity into the pre-selected missile, a process which is accomplished at the push of a button. This starts the missile 'thinking' about where it should fly. AMRAAM is then kicked free of the aircraft, ignites its Hercules rocket motor and zooms away in the general direction of the target using its Nortronics inertial mid-course guidance and microcomputer to guide it to the constantly computed intercept co-ordinates, steered by its 'flippers'. The options then open up: for a precise long-

◄ The Hughes AIM-120 AMRAAM became operational just in time for fifty-two rounds to be dispatched to Tabuk AB, Saudi Arabia, to equip the 58th TFS. One of the unit's Eagles is shown here being 'prepped' for a combat mission during February 1991.(DoD)

range shot, the launch jet continues to provide updates over a secure data-link until the missile's own miniature active radar dish acquires the target, freeing the launch fighter to 'knock it off'; alternatively, if the engagement is proving to be overbearing, the launch pilot can break away and trust that AMRAAM, once in the vicinity of the target, can go about its business and employ its seeker with the minimum of assistance; finally, at close quarters, AMRAAM's active seeker is locked on to the target prior to launch, permitting the attacker to effect immediate evasive manoeuvres.

The range at which autonomous missile lock-on can be accomplished in true fire-and-forget mode remains classified, but it is reported to be well beyond the capability of the latest 'Heat' weapons, and certainly BVR. Once launched, a second missile can be activated and assigned a fresh target, and so on, until as many as eight 'Fidos' (the maximum possible 'Zulu Alert' configuration for the F-15C Eagle) are whizzing through the sky on a collision course towards a like number of hapless enemy aircraft. The theory has been demonstrated successfully. A total of 89 pre-production and thirteen pilot production AIM-120As have been expended by the Joint System Program Office leaders of the USAF over the White Sands missile range in New Mexico and the Eglin, Florida-based

Gulf range, where the weapon has successfully created much scrap metal out of Sperry-adapted QF-100D target drones in circumstances which would leave the veteran 'Winder 'shooter' Walter Schirra flabbergasted. The climax of recent test shots witnessed the demolition by four independently guiding AMRAAMs of a quartet of tightly manoeuvring, unmanned, dayglo-orange 'Huns' which were pumping out volumes of chaff and radiating countermeasures in a vain attempt to foil the missiles; and the destruction of low-level drones which were attempting to use ground clutter in head-on encounters to mask their presence. Sustained turns of 28g were demonstrated.

'Fido' achieved IOC with the USAF's 58th TFS F-15Cs of the *Gulf Eagles* (the operational test force for AMRAAM, co-located at Eglin with the MSD) in time for deployment to Tabuk, Saudi Arabia, but none of the fifty-two rounds supplied was let off its leash. AMRAAM Program Director Brig. Gen. Charles Franklin noted that it was a matter of 'a shortage of trade' during the closing stages of the conflict, not reliability: 'From a reliability and performance standpoint, they wouldn't work well—they would work spectacularly!'. Capable of being carried on both Sidewinder and Sparrow launch rails, the slim AIM-120 is destined to oust Sparrow

▶ Hughes test pilot Chris Smith stands to attention between trials rounds of the AIM-47 Super Falcon and XAIM-54 Phoenix. The Super Falcon evolved from the AIM-4, while Phoenix in turn owes much to the active radar-equipped GAR-9. Both missiles possess only two sets of cruciform wings, comprising foreplanes and aft steering fins; the black lateral bands on the Super Falcon are deceptive. (Hughes Missiles)

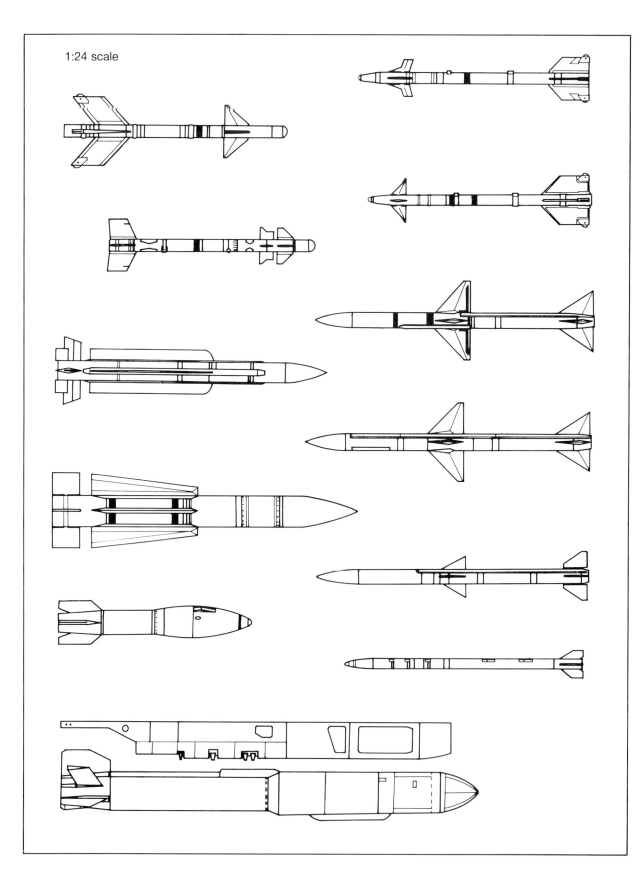

1:24 scale

▶ Seen here in its all-up Fleet Defense configuration, an F-14A from VF-32 *Swordsmen* makes a swept, high-speed pass with no fewer than six AIM-54C Phoenix bolted to its belly and glove pylons. The bigger carriers, such as the USS *Kennedy* from which this machine was operating, are long enough to accommodate a Tomcat in this configuration. The old *Midway* class 'flat-tops' (now retired from active duties) dictated a maximum load of four Phoenix, although a typical Tomcat load comprises a pair of Phoenix, two Sparrows and two Sidewinders. (Grumman Archives)

◀ Air-to-air missiles. Left, top to bottom: Python 3 heat-seeker; 550R Magic 2 heat-seeker (upside down in Jaguar overwing configuration); R530D Super SARH AAM; AIM-54C + Phoenix active radar-guided AAM; AIR-2A Genie nuclear gyro-stabilized AAM; and ASAT Anti-Satellite launcher and missile configuration as evaluated on the F-15A. Right, top to bottom: AIM-9P-3 Sidewinder heat-seeker; AIM-9L/M all-aspect Sidewinder (note the type's larger rear fins); AIM-7E-2 Sparrow III SARH AAM (the XJ521 Sky Flash and Aspide 1/1A are derived from this type); AIM-7F/M Sparrow III (note the long-chord electrical conduit); AIM-120A AMRAAM 'Fido'; and Raytheon 'flipper'-steered AIM-9X Sidewinder. (Author)

and Sky Flash in the armouries of the Eagle, Hornet, Phantom, Tomcat, Tornado and Viggen, to form the primary armament of the Gripen, and to equip the comparatively petite, radar-limited Harrier FRS.2 and F-16. Several Memoranda of Understanding (MoUs) have been signed with Britain, Germany and Sweden for co-production of the weapon in Europe to secure its progress. Follow-on growth is aimed at making the AMRAAM cheaper, less susceptible to the envisaged growth in countermeasures and much more stealthy so as to permit conformal carriage on the exterior of the emerging 'fourth-generation' low-observable fighters such as the Lockheed/Boeing/ General Dynamics F-22 'Lightning II', to bolster their overall firepower. Loral Aeronutronic is pursuing this line of thinking under Project 'Have Dash 2' and has already been contracted for a six-shot trials programme.

FROM THE ASHES

The king of all the fire-and-forget AAMs remains the Hughes AIM-54 Phoenix, named after the fabulous Arabian bird which, according to Greek legend, would build its own funeral pyre upon which it would reduce itself to ashes, only to rise once again, completely rejuvenated, to live for another 500 years. Hughes is not so bold as to claim that its air-to-air missile which goes by the same exotic title will endure for all time, but the name is indeed apt for a weapon which possesses remarkable airborne talents and which has survived a gruelling stop-go development cycle over the past three decades. In modern mythology, the Phoenix missile has become synonymous with US

naval supremacy. Launched from the belly or shoulder pylons of a competently crewed F-14 Tomcat (or 'Turkey') flying BARCAP, the weapon is capable of protecting sea-going battle groups from threats posed by both cruise missiles and aircraft by providing a defensive 'box' that encompasses a volume of a quarter-of-a-million cubic miles.

The AIM-54 Phoenix emerged from the growing piles of incinerated paperwork left by a number of promising but prematurely terminated weapons system programmes which had their genesis in the late 1950s as an adjunct to the then 'gee-whiz' Falcon series—the Hughes AIM-47 Super Falcon and AAM-N-10 Eagle, which were intended to equip the ill-fated North American F-108 Rapier, Douglas F6D Missileer and Lockheed F-12B Blackbird interceptors. A life-long companion to Phoenix, the allied AN/AWG-9 weapons control system and follow-on AN/APG-71 aircraft-mounted radars similarly evolved from earlier work carried out on integrated radar/missile packages.[10] The programme began life during 1962 in an effort to provide the Fleet with a sea-going stand-off missile system, initially intended for installation in the F-111B TFX-N (Tactical Fighter Experimental, Navy), before passing to the F-14A VFX (Navy Fighter Experimental) effort after 1967. The challenges Hughes faced were immense: the first operational application of fire-and-forget technology by means of a missile-mounted DSQ-26 active radar dish, the complexities of which have already been aired; multiple engagement capability from sea level up to an altitude of 100,000ft, at stand-off ranges of up to 130 miles; and a burn-out speed of Mach 5 matched to a big 133lb warhead—and all this within a 13ft long, 38in span missile! Hughes met the challenge head-on, with literally that goal in mind! They had also to turn around negative attitudes towards the comparatively diminutive Falcon and re-establish themselves in the marketplace. By 1966 their Culver City, California-based engineering team had perfected the 'brassboard' avionics and early test rounds, and on Thursday 12 May 1966 the first round was shot off from a Skywarrior test-bed to score a bull's-eye on a Ryan BQM-34 Firebee drone. During the great 'drone shoots' of the ensuing four years multiple shots against multiple targets were demonstrated, giving rise to the heading in the Phoenix system instruction manual: 'How to become an Ace on your first pass'! Targets skimming the waves at 50ft or flying at 103,000ft were felled with equal efficiency at launch ranges of up to 120 miles; while the AN/AWG-9 package proved capable of tracking up to two dozen targets and assigning Phoenix missiles according to the relative threat they presented. Pilots and their Radar Intercept Officers (RIOs; in those days known as Missile Control Officers) had merely to wait for 'In Range' lamp to light up before unleashing their deadly rocket cargo, which pulled manoeuvres of up to 17g to catch the inbound targets. The overall pK was 82 per cent.

Production of the complex Phoenix missile got underway during 1972, when the programme shifted east to the company's new plant at Tucson, Arizona. Early start-up problems were encountered and in April 1973 Navy Program Manager, Rear Admiral Leonard 'Swoose' Snead, visited the factory to emphasize the importance of getting the weapons rolling off the lines to feed his hungry new Tomcats, which would be taking to the skies with up to six missiles apiece. The personable Snead told the production engineers he had just chastised that he would like nothing more but to take back his criticisms '. . . and eat crow'. Hughes streamlined their production process while Snead's aides kept their noses pressed to the factory windows, and during a subsequent visit that August a very pleased 'Swoose' kept his word and ceremoniously bit into the neck of a stuffed raven! (A raven-shaped chocolate cake of Jane Asher ilk was quietly trolleyed in to ease 'Snead's' digestion!). Shortly afterwards, production

accelerated from a dozen to forty missiles a month, equipping the swelling ranks of F-14As at NAS Oceana, Virginia, and Miramar, California, which, under the auspices of VF-1 Wolfpack and VF-2 Bounty Hunters, made their inaugural cruise aboard the USS *Enterprise* from NAS Alameda in September 1974. This capability gave the US Navy an unparalleled air combat capability, making it the envy of the world. The sabre-rattling 'Any Time, Baby . . .' patch worn by Tomcat crews in various guises alludes to their stand-off missile capability, not to the rather underpowered swing-winged mount they fly. Such was the security value placed on the weapon that expensive salvage operations were mounted to retrieve any Tomcat that its crews had dared to abandon to the sea with a Phoenix bolted to its belly. 'Go down with it and keep an eye on it' was the stern but jocular briefing issued to all new fighter pilots growing accustomed to a second tail. The first such recovery took place in November 1976 at a cost of some $2 million following the loss of a 'Turkey' from VF-32 *Swordsmen* which had flopped off the deck of the USS *John F. Kennedy* near Scapa Flow.

Some 2,500 copies of the basic version were manufactured, including 484 for export to the type's sole foreign customer, Iran—also the only nation to have used the weapon in combat, as dictated by the exigencies of the bloody protracted war with Iraq, albeit in very limited numbers for want of qualified maintenance personnel and spares. For their own part, the US Navy's past forays into Colonel Qadafi's infamous 'Line of Death' have involved clashes with opponents well within 'eyeball' range as prescribed by the strict ROE, better suited to a Sparrow or Sidewinder volley. (And, during the Gulf War, the few Iraqi pilots prepared to run the American, Saudi and British gauntlet were caught by forward-emplaced flights of Eagles directed by AWACs; rearguard Tomcats performed BARCAP for the Fleet and maintained close ranks with the carrier fighter-bombers they were supporting, yet, had they been operational further north, they may well have thwarted the rush of hardware fleeing to Iran).

An AIM-54B model was under development by the end of the decade but, starting in 1981, production leapfrogged to 330 of the far superior 'Charlie' mark, which introduced solid-state electronics along with increased resilience to enemy jamming, improved

► A live AIM-54C-Plus Phoenix shows off its powerful lines at Hughes' plant in Tucson, Arizona. All but the radome, which is white, is painted in pale grey. The small bands are all steel-coloured; the front two large ones are yellow (representing a live warhead); and the after two, interrupted by the fins, are brown (denoting a live rocket motor). (Hughes Missiles)

target discrimination (both independent and 'netted') and a minimum range capability of 1.3 miles. Technological growth for technology's sake was one reason for the improvements. However, the real impetus was to keep US missile technology at least one step ahead of its potential foes, a situation exacerbated by the discovery that some Iranian supplies had been illicitly forwarded to the Soviet Union following the collapse of the Shah's regime. With some haste, US Navy stocks of the 'Alpha' variant received the updates during depot maintenance (a process to which missiles are subjected, on a similar basis to that of the jets they equip). Subsequent work aimed at further improving reliability led to the definitive C-Plus, which began to supplant its predecessor on the production lines in March 1986, while in the following year Raytheon joined Hughes as second-source supplier. Some 4,000 missiles remain in stock, with the final 420 Phoenix bought under FY 1991 contracts now nearing completion—enough to keep the Fleet's protective umbrella adequately supplied until the Tomcat becomes too long in the tooth to be maintained at the leading edge of US Navy air power. However, the intended replacement, the Advanced AAM (AAAM), until recently undergoing competitive development between the two teams Hughes/Raytheon and GD/Westinghouse, was axed in January 1992 as part of continuing defence cuts. The AAAM was to embody the range and all-altitude capabilities unique to the Phoenix with the dual-mode guidance employed by the definitive marks of Sparrow *and* the agility of AMRAAM—a demanding

set of specifications by anyone's reckoning!—so that the assignment of outer perimeter BARCAP could gradually pass over to advanced versions of the F/A-18E/F Hornet. It now seems that the Fleet will be obliged to forfeit this capability when the Tomcats begin to be phased out at the start of the new millenium.

SHOOTIN' IRONS

At the other end of the performance spectrum, as a fighter closes to well within visual range of its intended prey, the pilot switches to the guns: tried-and-trusted armament which predates the development of the fighter aircraft, when the radical Lewis, Spandau and Vickers were strictly earthbound and mounted on tripods. Although outmoded today with the advent of reliable fire-and-forget AAMs, they still are a useful weapon for use against targets of opportunity in the mêlée of a 'Fur Ball', and can be devastating when effectively employed for ground strafing. The big debates hinge upon which type is the most effective, and which calibre the optimum for all-round use. Western fighters customarily use one of only two general types—the General Electric 'Gatling' gun, or the Aden, DEFA, Mauser or Oerlikon cannon, all of which fall within the 20mm to 30mm calibre range.

The most widespread 'Gat' is the electrically driven GE 20mm M61A1, a six-barrel weapon which spins to spew out up to 7,200spm (shells per minute) at a muzzle velocity of 3,400fs—a far cry from Richard Jordan's original hand-cranked contraption! The M61A1 originated in 1949 at the com-

pany's Burlington, Vermont plant as the T-171, developed as a defensive sting-in-the-tail for the Boeing B-52H and General Dynamics B-58A. In deference to its project codename and the Roman god of fire, it has borne the title Vulcan ever since. It was introduced into service in 1958, its effectiveness soon became legendary and, in less than a decade, almost every US fighter during transition from the drawing board to an operational flight-line featured the system as standard internal equipment, plumbed into the aircraft's onboard electrical or hydraulic systems. For that notable exception the ubiquitous Phantom, produced as a gunless machine until May 1967, GE evolved the SUU-16/A, a RAT (ram air turbine) powered M61A1 contained in a 16ft pod, and its successor the SUU-23/A, which introduced the GAU-4 derivative. This drew on a portion of shell propellant gas to drive the barrels and, like its predecessor, was rated at the

6,000spm standard, with enough ammunition for up to twelve seconds of fire, typically shot off in 1–1½-sec bursts. Both the internal and external (podded) models possess their pros and cons. An internal mount drawing upon aircraft power offered a near-instant full rate of fire regardless of airspeed; its rigid fit created less 'dispersion' (making it a better air-to-air weapon); and it was designed to retain its spent shells, which were routed back to the ammunition drum. On the other hand, the spinning barrels would on occasion continue to send unspent shells through the linkless feed after the pilot had taken his finger off the trigger, placing them in close proximity with hot, spent cases, sometimes resulting in the whole assembly 'cooking off'.[11] By contrast, the SUU-16/A shed its spent cartridges through an exit slot, avoiding both 'cook off' and gun gas hazards, but at the expense of an angry Army and Marine Corps, whose troops, requesting overhead

▶ The F-111 featured an optional General Electric/Convair M61A1 20mm 'Gatling' gun 'pack' rated at 5,000spm, which could be bolted to the attack machine's capacious weapons bay—a philosophy later shared by the F-106A, which was endowed with a similar capability under Project 'Six Shooter'. Most other American aircraft of the era incorporated the M61A1 as a standard internal item, including the pioneers, the F-105B 'Thud' and F-104C Starfighter. (Frank B. Mormillo)

close-support (CAS) assistance, were frequently subjected to a downpour of warm brass! These were minor snags. Introduced to combat in South-East Asia aboard the USAF's Thai-based F-105D 'Thuds' and the Phantoms of the aptly nicknamed 366th TFW *Gunfighters*, by war's end the weapon had claimed a total of 32 MiGs, a surprisingly high

number of which were claimed by the fast but unmanoeuvrable F-105 'Lead Sleds'.

The 'Gat' became the standard gun for two generations of US-built fighters and is already slated to become standard equipment on the emerging F-22, yet it has always suffered one drawback—its inability to outgun the larger calibre 23–30mm cannon of

▶ Key subassemblies of the SUU-23/A 20mm 'Gatling' gun. (General Electric USA)

◀ A prettily painted SUU-23/A awaits a 'William Tell' shoot strapped to the starboard inboard pylon of a *Happy Hooligans* F-4D at Tyndall ADWC, Florida. The pods were usually carried on a rigid centreline mounting to reduce shell dispersion, but this inner-wing arrangement was adopted when the Phantoms acquired a new Fletcher/McDD Tulsa centreline fuel tank fit. Note also the 'blunt' rear fairing to the gun pod, which ensures adequate clearance for the Phantom's main undercarriage. (Mil-Slides)

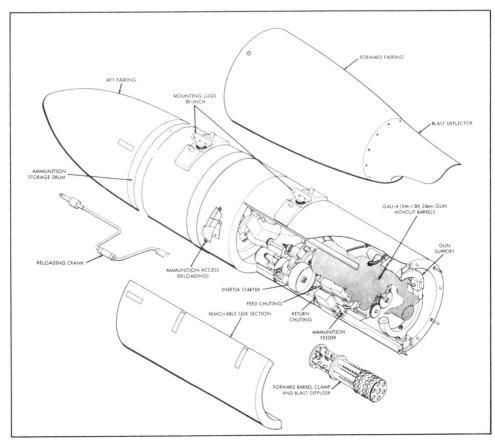

European origin, from both sides of the now-defunct 'Iron Curtain'. ACEVAL highlighted the need for a bigger 'Gat', ideally of 25mm calibre, and from this emerged the GE GAU-12/A Equalizer which equips the AV 8B Harrier II. However, every other fighter on the inventory keeps faith with the 20 'Mike-Mike' version, which remains extraordinarily reliable, having an average stoppage rate of less than one shell in 10,000. The anti-clockwise rotating sextet of rifled barrels reduces the normal wear and tear associated with a one-barrelled system, and with minor refurbishment each has a useful life of thirty years.[12]

However, the debate continues. For example, Oerlikon's Type KCA 30mm cannon, equipping the Viggen, the Mauser BK27 27mm, built into Tornado's nose, and the GIAT/DEFA 552–554 30mm series, arming the Mirage 'family', can really 'pump iron'. Muzzle velocity is comparable to that of the 'Gat' as cannon can each muster around 1,250spm, but what really sets them apart is their larger mass and the instantaneous full rates of fire available—a twentieth of a second as opposed to anything up to four-tenths of a second to get a 'Gat' into full

motion. Although these differences appear negligible given the overall rates of fire involved, it is contended by several tacticians that it is only when the hunter crosses paths with his prey that the aim is the *truest*: given the short bursts of fire customarily employed in these incredibly brief, almost intuitive, encounters and the response rates of cannon, they therefore offer a much higher pK, especially when two or more of them are brought to bear at once. Arguments to contradict this usually draw comparisons between the latest 'Gats' and obsolete guns such as the British Aden Mk. 4 and American Ford/Pontiac M39, both of which were based on German Second World War designs. The *Cheyl Ha'Avir*, which possesses more recent air combat experience than any other air arm, insists that a pair of traditional repeaters are preferable for air-to-air work, inasmuch as they offer the same punch at a much reduced weight.[13]

Unequivocally, it has been in the air-to-surface arena where the 'Gat' has truly excelled. American close air support experience in South-East Asia and the burgeoning threat of Soviet armoured formations in Europe under-

► Dassault's FLIR pod, developed for use on the Mirage 2000 series to give the crews night-time vision, dominates the camera frame. Also shown to good effect are a clutch of Matra Durandal boosted anti-runway munitions, plus the pilots' favourite weapon, the DEFA 30mm cannon installed as standard items in all *Chasseurs Français*. (Dassault)

◄ Feeding time for the A-10As of the 103rd TFG *Flying Yankees*, based at Bradley Field, Connecticut. The weapon loading system will replenish the 'Warthog's' GAU-8/A Avenger ammunition drum with 1,350 rounds of 30mm tank-busting shells. (Air National Guard Bureau)

lined the need for a 'shooter' capable of picking off thick-skinned tanks, and of destroying prickly AAA gunlaying armoured vehicles at arm's length. From this requirement was born GE's huge GAU-8/A 30mm Avenger. First demonstrated as the T-212 model in 1968 and subsequently tailored for Republic's dedicated armour-busting A-10A 'Warthog' (many rightly claim that the 'Hog' was designed *around* the Avenger), the system works on the same principles as its GAU-4/A Vulcan forebear but totes an impressive seven barrels set into motion by the aircraft's hydraulics. These are able to spit out 4,200spm, enough for 20 seconds' fire based on the 1,350-round drum squeezed into the aircraft. It is a formidable weapon. Its shells employ an aluminium body containing a depleted uranium 'slug', able to sustain their momentum over considerable distances; under normal conditions, the shells traverse 4,000ft in under 1.2 seconds, poking and shredding even mobile heavy armour. Interfaced with the new LASTE (Low Altitude Safety and Targeting Enhancement) modifications, which includes a new CCIP computer, the 'Hog's' Avenger can now reliably hit targets at slant ranges of 12,000ft. Ballistic 'fall off' is negligible also over this distance (around 10ft), and with judicious use of the rudder pedals the 'Hog' driver may 'spray' his targets with API (armour-piercing incendiary) or HEI (high-explosive incendiary) rounds. The weapon is equally adept at shredding enemy helicopters, and during the Gulf War a pair of 'Wart Eagles' scored the

only two gun kills of the conflict when they 'bagged' a couple of Iraqi rotorcraft. The only serious recurring problems encountered with the Avenger are its habit of demolishing strafing ranges even when using TP (target practice) ammunition, and the tendency for the powerful weapon to generate gas clouds which explode as 'fireballs' around the nose of the 'Hog' and cause residue to build up on the windshield (recently corrected by a retrofit programme which introduced a reconfigured muzzle deflector and additional gunbay gas-purge venting).

As a spin-off from the Avenger, GE has developed a four-barrelled gas-driven GAU-13/A model, packaged in a 13.8ft-long, 1,850lb Gepod designated the GPU-5/A. Because of its low recoil, it has been cleared for use on most land-based US fighter types (including such unlikely candidates as the OV-10 Bronco!). Carrying 353 rounds in its helical-feed casing, at 2,400spm the device can furnish a deadly 8.8 seconds of fire. 'Cook off' problems were eradicated from the outset by means of an auto-clearing system which reverses barrel rotation as soon as the pilot takes his finger off the 'pickle' button, to back all live rounds away from the hot spent cartridges (none of which is ejected on to the heads of 'friendlies'). The GPU-5/A entered service with the F-4D 906th TFG *Buckeye Phantoms* of the US Air Force Reserve (AFRes) at Wright-Patterson AFB, Ohio, in 1985 and has since gone on to become a mainstay F-16 anti-tank gunpod: the CAS-dedicated New York Air National

◄ Shown in its test livery of two-tone blue and white is the GE GPU-5/A Gepod, equipped with a four-barrelled GAU-4 variant of the Avenger. The pods, customarily painted olive green, are now the main weapon of the few F-16 units assigned to dedicated close air support duties. Amongst the first to field the pod on the 'Electric Jet' were the New York ANG's 174th TFW *The Boys from Syracuse*, which saw action in the Gulf while stationed at Al Kharj, Saudi Arabia. (General Electric)

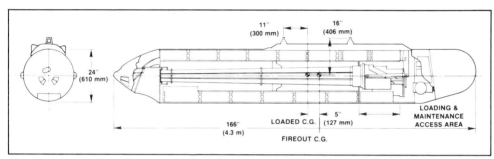

◄ Cut-away of the GPU-5/A Gepod, showing the four-barrelled gun and breech, plus the helical ammunition feed built into the pod's casing. (General Electric USA)

Guard's 174th TFW *Boys from Syracuse* were the first to form in the new role and saw battle in the Gulf (albeit without pods owing to the need to employ other weapons).[14]

The ultimate goal is to tie the larger-calibre, 25mm 'Gats' in with snap-shooting computers with a certain potential to track targets automatically through a limited arc of movement. According to a USAF officer, some impressive work with 'trainable' guns was done under the 'Fire Fly' programme, during which time the test force blew a manoeuvring F-86 drone out of the air with a mere four rounds! The ambitious effort then suddenly went 'black' (classified), indicating backroom application to the latest generation of stealth fighters. While many fighter pilots swear by the modern one-shot AAM, the gun remains a vital standby weapon with the potential for several bursts, and, if these developments are anything to go by, it has plenty of tricks left up its sleeve!

NOTES TO CHAPTER ONE

1. Phase-out took place shortly before the 120th FIG, Montana ANG, traded in its sleek 'Sixes' for F-16A/B ADFs. An ATR-2A training version—developed under Project 'Ting-a-Ling', an offshoot from 'Ding-Dong'—was available, which blew up into a large white smokeball. The apt but silly codenames were deliberate, in an effort to play down the missiles' importance.
2. GAR stood for Guided Aerial Rocket (cf. the AIR-2 Genie, a simple Aerial Intercept Rocket), and was applied to all USAF guided AAMs prior to the US DoD overhaul of all three services' weapons systems designations in the autumn of 1962. The GAR-1 to -4 Falcon thence became the AIM-4 and the GAR-8 Sidewinder the AIM-9.
3. See Chapter 3 for more details regarding the Maverick. Falcon offshoots, the AIM-47 and AIM-54 Phoenix, are discussed below. The much-misunderstood Falcon remains active in the role of electronic warfare development. For example, during 1990, 54 AIM-4Gs were fired at a cliff face at White Sands, New Mexico, to evaluate the effectiveness of a brassboard Missile Approach Warning System (MAWS, which is discussed in the closing paragraphs of Chapter 5). A few are also believed to be in standby storage with the JASDF F-4EJ interceptor forces of Japan.
4. Described below. Shortly after receiving brand new F-4D Phantoms in May 1967 equipped with AIM-4D Falcons, Col. Robin Olds, leader of the famous Ubon-based 8th TFW *Wolfpack* in Thailand, ordered them removed and substituted by the tried-and-trusted Sidewinder!
5. The SARH Super 530F introduced a 9,000m

snap-up capability, completely revised aerofoils, a burnout speed of Mach 4.6 and a (classified) range estimated at 30 miles. It entered service in December 1979 with the Mirage F1 interceptor forces. The MICA is destined to enter service this decade and takes the concept yet a stage further, using thrust-vectoring as well as canard steering, plus a fire-and-forget capability akin to that of the AIM-120 AMRAAM (see below). An infra-red version of MICA is also envisaged.

6. The USAF uses argon gas cooling contained within the missile round; the US Navy utilizes nitrogen cooling fed from the launch rails. The only other major deviation in the series was the Motorola-built AIM-9C, which used SARH, matched to the Magnavox radar of the F-8 Crusader. These have subsequently been adapted into the radar-homing AGM-122A Sidearm for the defence-suppression mission. See Chapter 3.

7. Precursors to Red Top during Britain's all too brief efforts with heat-seeking AAMs included the Firestreak, developed as Project 'Blue Jay', which achieved IOC during 1958 with the Royal Navy's Sea Venoms of 893 NAS and with the RAF's Javelin interceptors of No. 33 Squadron. The weapon packed a hefty 50lb warhead and was followed by 'Red Top' (né Firestreak Mk. IV), which entered service with the RAF's Lightning F.3s of No. 74 (Tiger) Squadron and with the RN Sea Vixens of 899 NAS during 1964. The last of the latter, which featured impressive 68lb warheads, were withdrawn from service shortly after 30 April 1988 when the last Lightning unit, No. 11 Squadron, based at RAF Binbrook, stood down from NATO air defence duties.

8. Refer to 'Shootin' Irons', below. A means of addressing the identification problem has been to introduce long-range E-O sensors slaved to radar, such as the Northrop TISEO (Target Identification System Electro-Optical) which equips F-4Es built after the summer of 1972, and the same company's more sophisticated TCS (Television Camera Set) now fitted as standard to F-14 Tomcats. Less sophisticated equivalents embrace the plug-in telescopic viewfinders equipping the RAF's dwindling numbers of FGR.2 Phantoms and selected USAF F/15C Eagles. E-O imagers are discussed in Chapter 5 in the context of air-to-surface systems.

9. Causing some misunderstandings about the optimum use of Sparrow, which prevail today. In the mid-1970s, Sparrow's short-range capability became the focus of attention of the US Congressional General Accounting Office which was evaluating the need for such (now long since abandoned) efforts as the short-to-medium range XAIM-82A DAAM (Dogfight AAM) and XAIM-95

Agile, which had by then reached the hardware stage in development. Another casualty was the XAIM-97 Seekbat, a heat-seeking version of the AGM-78 STARM—see Chapter 3.

10. Beginning with the MG-3/10 and MA-1 systems installed in the Convair 'Deuce' and 'Six' and followed by the AN/ASG-18 of the Rapier and F-12B. These were tied to the NORAD SAGE system (or NADGE equivalent in Europe). The US Navy AN/AWG-9 adopted a similar approach by linking the aircraft, its radar and its Phoenix missiles directly to the carrier's control centre and to the terminals of E-2 Hawkeye airborne early warning aircraft, though target 'prioritization' ultimately remained the responsibility of the fighter crew. The F-101Bs, F-102As and F-106As of yesteryear were considered a mere manned extension of the air defence system.

11. The F-111A, for example, which could be configured with a Convair/GE M61A1 'Gat Pack' in its weapons bay, had to be downrated to 5,000spm after a trials machine's gunbay blew up. The long-term engineering fix was to introduce auto-clearing systems. See below.

12. A whole range of 'Gats', ranging in size from the 7.62mm 'minigun' to the 20mm Vulcan, equip Combat Search and Rescue helicopters and both rotary- and fixed-wing gunships. Their use in South-East Asia gave rise to aircraft nicknames like 'Spooky' and 'Puff the Magic Dragon', after it was discovered that some peasant Viet Cong thought that they were being assaulted by dragons: by night, when tracer rounds were used, the guns created violent bolts of orange-red fire.

13. The *Cheyl Ha'Avir* tested this theory by re-equipping a solitary F-4E *Kurnass* with a pair of DEFA 30mm cannon. Costs, and the marginal benefits involved, precluded a full-scale refit. The weight/size issue of the 'Gat' installation was critical to small fighters such as the Mirage III and its illicitly manufactured protégés, the Nesher and Kfir. For identical reasons, the only modern US fighter to incorporate cannon has been the diminutive Northrop F-5E Tiger/F-20A Tigershark series.

14. Principally the Maverick, *ibid*. The F-16As introduced a lot of new devices to battle during 'Desert Storm', including the Rockwell-Collins CP-1516/ASQ Automatic Target Handoff System (ATHS), which enabled forward air controllers—usually 'Killer Scout' F-16Cs equipped with precision GPS Navstar position receivers and ATHS handoff systems—to relay target co-ordinates directly into the *Syracusians'* bombing computers.

2.
ASSISTED BY GRAVITY

'**A** BOMB is a bomb, and hasn't changed much since World War One in terms of the hole it makes in the ground'. Even in the recent past, this sentiment perhaps held some truth, but those words bear little relation to today's conventional munitions, which are almost as diverse as their designations.

The great catalyst for the development of purpose-designed 'hole-makers' emerged during World War Two, when it was discovered that the weapons were far more effective when fuses, casings and warhead designs were matched to the assigned targets—a science known to today's air crews as 'weaponeering'. This realization has spawned not only a wide variety of bomb types since those days—penetrating, area, cluster and combined-effects munitions (CEM), and fuel-air explosives (FAE), often built around 'families' of canisters—but a cornucopia of shapes optimized for specific delivery tactics (medium-to-high or low altitude, high or low speed, glide and pure freefall) and, today, for stealth. One of the first major strides forward, however, was the development of streamlined munitions compatible with the new fast jets, which toted their ordnance externally in an effort to maximize much-needed internal fuel capacity.[1]

BASIC 'IRONWARE'
The United States, and the Douglas Aircraft Company in particular, with a blossoming stake in turbojet air power, was the first to address the need. Its sporty little A-4 'Scooter', the harbinger of many exciting technologies,[2] provided the impetus for change. Beginning in 1946 and working in concert with the US Navy Bureau of Aeronautics, Douglas evolved the Mark 80 series of Aero-1A conical-shaped Low Drag General Purpose (LDGP) bombs. These featured a tapered 8:3 aspect ratio—the

optimum compromise between low drag and a useful warhead—which ranged in size and yield from the seldom used Mk. 81, jokingly referred to as the 'Firecracker', through to the huge Mk. 84 'Hammer' which can blast out 8,500 cubic feet of earth and shatter eardrums half a mile distant. Utilizing heavy steel, prefragmented cases with a comparatively modest quantity of H6, Minol 2 or Tritonal explosives (which account for about 50 per cent of the bomb's all-up weight), the series was designed to do its job using a combination of fragmentation and blast, much like an air-delivered 'super grenade'.

Entering service in the late 1950s in four LDGP varieties known as 'slicks'—the Mk. 81 250lb, Mk. 82 500lb, Mk. 83 1,000lb and Mk. 84 2,000lb—the 'family' was soon adopted by the USAF and subsequently by many foreign air arms, many of whom produce the

▶ After a lapse of nineteen years of peacetime operations, including reassignment to full-time conventional strike and frequent 'Busy Brewer' forays to RAF Fairford in England, the venerable B-52G was once more thrown into combat in early 1991, evoking fifty-year-old memories of the 8th Air Force. Fairford's wartime 806th Bomb Wing (Provisional) drew on 'Buffs' from the 2nd, 93rd, 379th and 416th Bomb Wings, and flew most of its strikes with Mk. 82 'slicks' (seen clutched under the wings of 'What's Up Doc?', taking to the skies) and M117s (lined up on the trailer in the second shot). (Peter E. Davies)

◀ A clear case of how important 'weaponeering' is to modern combat aircraft! Two determined-looking RAAF crewmen stand astride a hefty quantity of ordnance available to that Service's swing-wing F-111C 'Aardvark'. Behind the 20mm 'Gatling' gun ammunition lie Mk. 82 'slick' and Snakeye 500lb bombs, AIM-9B Sidewinders, GBU-12 LGBs, BL755s with 'slick' tails and AGM-84 Harpoons, plus Mk. 84 'hammers' and their 'smart' derivatives the GBU-10 and -15. (RAAF)

series under licence to the United States or have developed indigenous equivalents (some of which have since trickled into squadron use by former Eastern Bloc countries). For example, Cardoen in Santiago manufactures the series for the *Fuerza Aerea de Chile* and Explosivos Alaveses in Spain builds licenced copies for the *Ejercito del Aire Espanol*. Despite the other advances mentioned in this essay, this popular, inexpensive selection will probably be around for as long as warplanes exist to carry them.

The Mk. 80 series was backed by a pair of USAF designs, the M117 750lb and M118 3,000lb bombs, which fulfilled the need for bombs of a larger yield, as is permissible when employing the luxury of a long, straight runway in which to get airborne. These have similarly been adopted by numerous overseas allies and FMS customers, and manufactured overseas also at such far-flung locations as South Korea and Israel. In con-

junction with the Mk. 80 series, they form a 'common six' which can be adapted by ground crews into a number of sub-models. The most notable variations are the high-drag versions, designed for low-level deliveries where the attacker can otherwise all too easily get caught in the debris-laden blast of its own ordnance. These substitute the 'slick' tail with a 'pop-open' steel cruci-form arrangement to create the M117R and Mk. 82 Mod. 1, the famous 'Retarder' and Snakeye, respectively. Fuses also vary con-siderably, from the now widely used M904 and FMU-54 (Fuse, Munitions Unit) impact fuses (the basic bomb), through the FMU-26, -72 and -139 delayed-action fuses (turning the weapons into mines), to the FMU-113 proximity detonator (designed for air burst, to maximize the bomb's effect against disper-sed targets; a poor man's way to get a similar effect was to put an M904 on the end of a 36in pipe, a method originating in the

◄ The 750lb M117 'iron' bombs carried by the 'Buffs' featured traditional wartime chalked graffiti, some of which speaks for itself! Note that these bombs have the 'long' low-drag fins installed, typical of Israeli M117s also. (Tim Perry)

► Mk. 82 Snakeyes equipped with the steel retarding fins are used for low-level bombing. The fins pop open into a cruciform air brake configuration to prevent the attacker from being shredded in the blast of its own ordnance but impose a 500kt deliery speed limitation. This spurred development of the Loral 'Ballute'. (Robin A. Walker via Peter E. Davies)

◄ One of the West's best multi-role fighters is the McAir F-15E Eagle, nicknamed the 'Mud Hen', 150 of which are entering service with the newly reorganized USAF Air Combat Command's European and Contingency Forces. Four machines from the two Luke, Arizona-based training squadrons, the 461st *Deadly Jesters* and 550th *Silver Eagles*, fly in echelon equipped with conformally carried Mk. 82 LDGP 'slicks' and shoulder-mounted AIM-9L/M Sidewinders. (McAir)

Vietnam War, to make a 'Daisy Cutter'). These subtle alterations create a whole new range of bombs, such as the Snakeye Mk. 36 DST (Destructor), which can be fitted with magnetic or seismic fuses and set off by a passing vehicle. The combinations are almost endless. In South-East Asia, US Navy crews became particularly adept at employing the Mk. 82 in all these guises (this warhead being the most popular in the 'family', accounting for 90 per cent of the total tonnage dropped in the theatre) and devised their own names for the various bombs and missions, all with a distinctively horticultural flavour: for example, regular Mk. 82 Snakeyes might be dropped on a suspected stretch of the Ho Chi Minh Trail in Laos to churn up the earth—the so-called 'Rotortiller' missions—before sensors and Mk. 36 DSTs were 'planted' or 'seeded' in the prepared earth. Thus, what looks like merely two or three types of bomb in fact comprises a huge range from which the 'weaponeers' can mix and match, according to mission requirements.[3]

SAFETY

Combat experience during and since Vietnam has given rise to some important, though subtle, changes. The US Navy, caught in three major conflagrations aboard its carriers *Oriskany* (26 October 1966), *Forrestal* (29 July 1967) and the nuclear-powered *Enterprise* (14 January 1969), prompted a major rethink. A magnesium flare accidentally set off and tossed into the hold was blamed for the first incident, but the lat-

ter two occurred in identical circumstances—5in Zuni rockets triggered into action on a crowded deck, possibly as a consequence of electronic interference from starters and radars (a problem tentatively identified as HERO, or Hazards of Electromagnetic Radiation to Ordnance). As well as many injured sailors and aviators, these tragedies resulted in 196 men losing their lives, 38 aircraft being destroyed and repair bills amounting to a quarter of a billion dollars. One ameliorator was to coat the Service's bombs—the chief weapons to be found on deck and snuggled in the ships' magazines—in a thick, textured layer of ablative material, which prevents them from 'cooking off' in the event of a blaze; instead, they merely fizzle away, giving firefighters and their assistants plenty of time in which to lob the weapons overboard. To this day, US Navy bombs are readily identified by their ready-mix surface coat and twin yellow nose bands.

Improvements to the fuses have been effected for precisely the opposite reason. During the Falkland Islands campaign, the British Fleet were thankful that many of the Argentine Mk. 82s failed conspicuously as a result of malfunctions or because the bombs were dropped from below their fuse-related 200ft minimum, thereby preventing the air-driven M904 vanes from arming the weapons properly prior to impact. Many Mk. 82s were simply rendered harmless and booted overboard! Had updated bombs been dropped, the outcome of the entire conflict may have been terrifyingly different.

◀ Mk. 82 bombs may be fitted with nose or tail fuses (or both) and these are 'safed' using steel wire. When the bomb is released from its rack the wire snaps, freeing the vanes to turn and arm the bomb. These two views depict US Navy and Air Force crews demonstrating the 'safing' process. Note also the twin-versus-single nose bands employed by the two services, and the rough, textured finish of the Navy ordnance. (DoD)

◀ In the early 1980s the USAF began to replace the Mk. 82 LDGP and Snakeye tail 'groups' with the new Loral (then Goodyear Aerospace) BSU-49 'Ballute', so named because when deployed in the retarded mode it employs a balloon-cum-parachute; the all-up configuration is known as the Mk. 82 AIR. In crisp focus here, several are seen strapped to a weapons trolley ready for loading aboard A-7Ds from the 121st TFW, Ohio ANG, preparatory to a 'Gunsmoke 87' bomb competition sortie at Nellis TFWC, Nevada. (Frank B. Mormillo)

◀ The 'Ballute' in action, dropped from a drab grey-green A-7D over the Nellis ranges. The weapons were used in combat for the first time in April 1986 when F-111Fs of the 48th TFW *Statue of Liberty Wing* struck Tripoli Airport. (LTV)

▲ An F-111E of the 20th TFW demonstrates the high-altitude bombing technique which it used so effectively when operating from Incirlik AB, Turkey, under the command of the 4770th Combat Wing (the first 'Super Wing' to be created and tested in war). In addition to dropping Mk. 82 LDGP bombs, the units (composed of elements from the 55th TFS *Fightin' Fifty-Fifth*, 77th TFS *Gamblers* and 79th TFS *Tigers*) also deposited Mk. 84s and CBU-87 and -89 cluster bombs. A total of 413 combat sorties were flown, without loss. (USAFE)

Undoubtedly the greatest stride forward for the humble Mk. 80 'iron' bomb series has been the creation of the Loral (formerly Goodyear) 'Ballute'. This marries the familiar trio of Mk. 82, 83 and 84 with an appropriate dual-mode, spring-activated, balloon-cum-parachute tail, nicknamed the 'Ballute' but more correctly referred to as the Air Inflatable Retard (AIR). The roots of this long overdue update, which has recently superseded the Snakeye in USAF service, lie in combat experience. Snakeye possessed a 500kt air-speed limitation, beyond which the cruciform air brakes were liable to malfunction, the obvious consequence of which was that an attacking jet would get shredded by its own munitions. Pilots flying the new-range tran-sonic attackers such as the F-4 and F-111 were obliged to throttle back during the hair-raising attack run, an undesirable situation in

the light of their motto which proclaimed that 'Speed is Life!'. The new AIR, by contrast, imposes no such limitations and is capable of, in the words of former 'Vark' pilot Maj. Dick Brown, being 'dropped as low as 100ft at the speed of heat—as fast as the old jet will go. The 2,000lb version is particularly impressive—[the] best bomb we've got. Just drop it and it makes a mini-mushroom!'. Until the advent of the 'Ballute', the Mk. 84 model was available only in 'slick' format, forcing the attacker to pull up off the target in reheat, which exposed it to the full fury of the enemy's defences. Set to remain stored, 'Ballutes' may also be employed from altitude or in high-angle dive-bombing, just like the old LDGP models. The Mk. 82 AIR first flexed its muscles during the United States' retaliatory attacks against Libya in April 1986, and the Mk. 84 AIR was used in massive quantities during 'Desert Storm' five years later. Overseas recipients included Royal Saudi Air Force Tornado GR.1s.

PENETRATORS AND SLEDGEHAMMERS

One of the chief drawbacks of all these 'iron' bombs is an inherent weakness as a result of their being designed for fragmentation. Mass-produced as steel casts like giveaway souvenirs, they have a tendency to break up on impact with hardened targets, doing little more than create a lot of noise. Immediately following the Arab-Israeli clash of October 1973, when the Americans and Soviets vied vicariously for military superiority on and over the war-torn Sinai Desert and Golan Heights, tensions between East and West approached breaking point for the third time since the Berlin Crisis and every military installation or piece of kit worth protecting, on both sides, was either buried under-ground beneath thick reinforced concrete or

FUSES

Fuse	Nose/ Tail	Type	Notes
General-purpose bombs			
M904	N	Instantaneous or short delay	
M905/ATU-35	T	Instantaneous or short delay	
Mk. 43	N	Proximity	High-drag bombs only
FMU-26	N/T	Instantaneous or short delay	
FMU-54	T	Instantaneous	
FMU-72	N/T	Long delay	
FMU-113	N	Proximity	Replaces old 'Daisy Cutter'
FMU-139	N/T	Instantaneous or short delay	
Paveway options			
M905/ATU-35	T	Short delay	Paveway I series
FMU-26	N/T	Short delay	Paveway I series
FMU-81	N/T	Short delay	Paveway II/III series
FMU-139	N/T	Instantaneous or short delay	Paveway II/III series
FMU-143	T	Instantaneous or short delay	Penetration warheads
Cluster bomb dispensers			
M907 and FMU-26	N	Time delay	SUU-30
Mk. 339	N	Time delay	SUU-30 and Mk. 20
FMU-56	N	Proximity	SUU-30
FMU-110	N	Proximity	SUU-30
FZU-39	N	Proximity	SUU-64 and -65

◄ One of the most impressive 'dumb' bombs available is the Mk. 84 AIR, which marries a one-ton 'hammer' with the Loral BSU-50 'Ballute'. The F-111F 'Tack Vark' in the background may carry four of them at a time, and drop them at 200ft 'at the speed o' heat'. (Peter E. Davies)

provided with its own blast-proof shell, replete with filters and scrubbers to prevent contamination from nuclear, biological and chemical (NBC) weaponry. Drab grey hardened aircraft and armour shelters sprouted like fungi at all key military installations while senior staff and their command and control functions burrowed inexorably further underground, rendering most of the old 'iron' bombs ineffectual. Short of deploying extra quantities of tactical nuclear weapons to forward locations to address the tougher potential targets, an option which was becoming increasingly politically unpalatable (though put into limited effect all the same), the only course was to field a new range of weapons: ones possessing mind-boggling precision and toughened warheads

◄ Oxford Blue 25lb BDU-33 (Mk. 76) 'slick' practice bombs emulate the ballistic characteristics of the full-sized LDGP weapons such as the Mk. 80 series so are used far more often than the all-up items, or than their concrete-filled BDU-50 equivalents (more commonly known as 'inert Mk. 82s'). The open-bottomed SUU-20/A dispenser is in wide service in the United States and has provision for the seldom-used FFAR rockets. (Frank B. Mormillo)

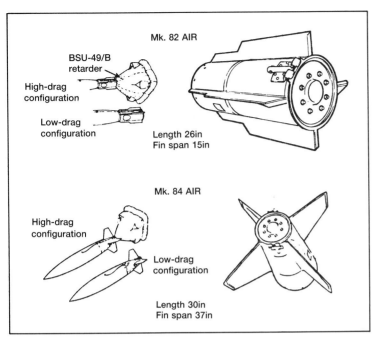

Mk. 82 AIR

BSU-49/B retarder

High-drag configuration

Low-drag configuration

Length 26in
Fin span 15in

Mk. 84 AIR

High-drag configuration

Low-drag configuration

Length 30in
Fin span 37in

▲ The Loral BSU-49/B and -50/B tails can be fitted to the Mk. 82 and Mk. 84 'iron' bomb series to create the 'Ballute'. A BSU-85/B version is also available for the US Navy Mk. 83. (USAF)

dams and cleaved hefty submarine pens and viaducts—the Ministry of Defence produced specifications which became ever more stringent. The gargantuan ancestors died alongside the great V-bomber force, but their little protégés are prolific, and the RAF currently enjoys access to a standard range of 1,000lb munitions encased in forged steel, each manufactured to an extremely high tolerance, and capable of causing considerable mischief. Built by Royal Ordnance (now a division of BAe), these comprise the Mk. 10, 13, 18 and 20 warheads mated to 'slick' Type 107 and 114 or Hunting No. 117 (retarder) fins, for high-, medium- or low-altitude delivery, very much in line with the American philosophy but packing a harder punch. During the course of Operation 'Granby', the RAF dropped more than 2,000 of these weapons, over half of which, drawn from Mk. 13/18 stocks, had been adapted into 'smart' models.[5] Perhaps the greatest accolade came from the American B-52G crews of the 4300th Wing, who with a wide grin on their faces described the 1,000-pounders, painted appropriately enough in gloss British Racing Green, as 'super!' The seventy 'Buffs' flying from Jeddah in Saudi Arabia, Moron AB in Spain, RAF Fairford in England and Diego Garcia in the Indian Ocean were on several occasions each tasked to drop a string of three dozen of these bombs at a time. It is

which would do more than merely spoil the paintwork and lay bare the grass knolls covering these complexes.[4]

The RAF, for its own part, had been well aware of this for decades and maintained a lead. Drawing on its wartime tradition with the great concrete-smashers—the Barnes Wallis-inspired 'bouncing bomb' and the 22,000lb 'Grand Slam', which cracked open

▶ Working up in the USA preparatory to its deployment to the 'Heath' in April 1992, an F-15E in 48th TFW markings wings its way over the Florida test range with a set of conformally mounted Mk. 84 AIRs. (USAFE)

◄ These propaganda leaflets were three of many types dropped on Iraqi positions during 'Desert Storm'. Their message is clear: 'This is the beginning! Perhaps these will be real bombs [next time]!'

believed that a handful of these were of the latest 'earthquake' variety, with the charges designed to focus their shockwaves in a seismic array to cause the enemy underground enclaves to implode. However, the crews remain coy on this subject: the security surrounding the latest British bombs remains extremely tight.

Not to be outdone, the United States has also for some years been developing a brand new range of warheads encased in forged, tempered steel cylinders designed specifically to negate heavily reinforced defences, the latest of which is the $13,000 Improved-2000, developed by the Lockheed Space & Missiles Company under Project 'Have Void' as an adjunct to the 'Have Blue' and 'Senior Trend' efforts from which hatched the extraordinary F-117 stealth bomber. Designated BLU-109/B, the one-ton bomb, made up of 75 per cent steel and only 25 per cent explosives, has supplanted the Mk. 84 in a number of tactical and pseudo-strategic roles, yet was originally conceived as a 'special mission' device to be used exclusively for covert strikes in support of US Army Rangers and Delta Force squads—the raison d'être of the F-117 too, before Congress swelled Lockheed's order books and created a Tactical Wing's worth of the radical $100 million attack machines. The 'void' in the remainder of the tac-air community's ordnance 'igloos' was subsequently stocked when the advantages of the new device became apparent during drops from F-4 Phantoms over the Eglin Range in Florida. Little were Lockheed to know that, eight years later, during the height of the air war in the Persian Gulf, an average year's production run of 2,500 units would be guzzled up every twelve days!

The BLU-109/B is customarily adapted into one of several different 'smart bomb' configurations, to be hung externally under the F-15E and F-111F, or to be nestled in the capacious belly of the F-117A.[6] When released from medium to high altitudes, the weapon generates sufficient kinetic striking power to punch through over 12ft of reinforced concrete prior to detonation, and it can be used effectively at oblique strike angles of up to 60°.

If area punch matters most, then, short of

► Painted in its startling blue and golden yellow chequered livery, a Jaguar GR.1 from No. 54 Squadron based at RAF Coltishall departs with a duo of Royal Ordnance 1,000lb 'iron' bombs. The live versions are painted in gloss British Racing Green; the inert examples used for weapons loading practice and full-sized dummy drops are painted Oxford Blue. (Author)

employing tactical nuclear weapons, the next best option is the huge American 'Tarzans', developed just prior to the Korean War as radio-controlled 12,000lb VB-13 monsters, whose basic warheads were frequently rolled out of the cargo bay of transports to make large holes in the Vietnamese jungle canopy in order to create instant helicopter landing zones. There are few aircraft today which have the capacity to carry these, but there is one very unusual customer—the MC-130E/H 'Combat Talon' Hercules assigned to the

Special Operations Command, whose head-quarters are at Hurlburt Field in Florida. These machines, noted by their Fulton STARS proboscises and beefy structure optimized for low-level, covert, infiltration/ex-filtration missions by night and adverse weather, were equipped with pallets capable of jettisoning the gargantuan 15,000lb BLU-82/B, a high-capacity, light-case (HCLC) weapon which was rolled out of the rear cargo hatch. In contrast to the smaller Mk. 80 series, the HCLC comprises a high propor-tion of explosive—80 per cent's worth—so that the blast effect from these bombs is staggering: when fitted with a 4ft 'Daisy Cut-ter' for detonation above ground level, the weapon annihilates anything sitting on the ground within a 3–4 mile radius! Eleven BLU-82s were dropped over enemy troop posi-tions by the 'Combat Talons' during 'Desert Storm', along with graffiti, some of which proclaimed that more BLU-82/Bs were on the way. They took a terrible toll on Iraqi morale, living up to the nickname given to the weapon by the crews who flew the drops out of Riyadh and King Abdul Aziz air bases in Saudi Arabia: 'The mother of all bombs! Those survivors who popped out their bunkers like prairie dogs following such an aerial onslaught would discover that their armour and guns had been "trashed", as if a giant hand had swept across the desert'.

SPRINKLERS AND FIRE BOMBS

To the men from Royal Ordnance who, as these words are being written, have the unenviable, tedious and dangerous job of clearing Kuwait of unexpended munitions by hand, they are known as 'Baby Rockeyes' or

'DUMB' AND 'SMART' BOMBS

Basic 'iron' bomb	Approx. weight (lb)	High-drag and 'smart' adaptations
Mk. 82 'slick'	500	Snakeye with metal pop-open retard tail AIR with BSU-49 Ballute retard tail GBU-12A/B Paveway I LGB, high- and low-speed GBU-12B-D/B Paveway II LGB GBU-22/B Paveway III LLLGB
M117 vintage	750	M117R with metal pop-open retard tail KMU-342 with experimental Paveway LGB fit
Mk. 83 'slick'	1,000	AIR with BSU-85 Ballute retard tail GBU-16/B Paveway II LGB AGM-123A Skipper II rocket-assisted LGB
Mk. 84 'slick'	2,000	AIR with BSU-50 Ballute retard tail GBU-8/B Hobos EOGB I GBU-10/B or A/B Paveway I LGB, high- and low-speed GBU-10C-E/B Paveway II LGB GBU-15(V)1/B EOGB, with wide-chord MXU-724 fins GBU-15(V)2/B EOGB, with short-chord MXU-787 fins GBU-24/B Paveway III LLLGB AGM-130 rocket-assisted GBU-15(V)2/B
BLU-109/B	2,000	GBU-10G-J/B Paveway II LGB GBU-24A/B Paveway III LLLGB GBU-27A/B Paveway III seeker, Paveway II tail GBU-15(V)32 EOGB, with short-chord MXU-787 fins AGM-130I rocket-assisted GBU-15I
M118 vintage	3,000	GBU-9/B Hobos EOGB I GBU-11A/B Paveway I LGB

◀ Guardsmen raise a Rockeye cluster bomb into position with the assistance of an MJ-1 'Jammer'. Based on Mk. 7 dispenser canisters, Rockeyes are overall gloss white with a copper-coloured fuse 'rosette'. The USAF employed the Mods. 3 and 4 types in the Gulf, the US Navy using Mod. 6 types also, which feature twin nose bands. (Mike Holloway)

'Bloos'; to the Iraqi troops lucky enough to have survived an attack, they are referred to by the more sinister yet poignantly poetical name 'Black Rain': tiny bomblets that were scattered over the battle area from air-delivered canisters. Known officially as Cluster Bomb Units (CBUs) and used widely for the first time by US forces in South-East Asia, by the late 1980s the 'family' had evolved into ever more lethal packages. Their task is simple: to spread as much firepower as possible over a large area to disrupt, destroy and demoralize enemy ground forces, without having to resort to 'overkill'.

Amongst the best known is the Mk. 20 Rockeye II, developed by the US Naval Weapons Center at China Lake from 1963 and entering full-scale production four years later. This is built around a 7½ft-long Mk. 7 canister and has been gradually adapted into a number of configurations, all of which are capable of being dropped from as low an altitude as 250ft and of saturating (when fused to split and dispense its terrible cargo at 500ft) an area of up to 3,333 square yards. Its numerous sub-configurations comprise the basic Mk. 20 Mod. II, which contains 247 M118 anti-tank munitions designed to destroy armour on impact; the CBU-59/B APAM, which boasts a hefty load of 717 BLU-77/B anti-personnel, anti-*matériel* bomblets; and the CBU-78/B, composed of a mixture of 29 BLU-91/B anti-personnel and 38 BLU-92/B Gator anti-tank mines which

arm on reaching the ground and are then set off by magnetic influences or tripwire whiskers. External differences between the various 'Rockeyes' are few, and the latest variation on the theme, also outwardly indistinguishable from its partners at a distance, is the ISCB-1, designed by the major Rockeye builders ISC Technologies. This works as an area-denial system by scattering 65 dummy and 160 electrically timed live mines, the latter preset to go off at any time within 24 hours of self-arming. Rockeyes have been adopted by many NATO countries and were one of the key weapons deposited on the hapless Iraqi forward formations.

Other CBUs which are in widespread use include a range of devices based on the SUU-30H/B canister. These can be filled with anything from innocuous leaflets to razor-like *flechettes*, ball-bearings or other lethal fragments packed in tennis ball-sized bomblets bearing the 'salad bowl' names 'Guava', 'Orange' and 'Grapefruit' and charged with such nasty substances as zirconium, 'Composition B' and cyclotrol. Their job is to 'shred' soft targets such as AAA guns, radar dishes and trucks—and people. The newest of all are the CBU-87/B CEM and CBU-89/B Gator, both based on the bigger SUU-64 or -65 Tactical Munitions Dispensers (TMDs). The CEMs are so designed that on hitting a soft target they simply blow up like a grenade; but on contact with a hard target, such as a tank hull, the core of the miniature

▶ The SEAD (suppression of enemy air defences) mission makes extensive use of cluster bombs, which are highly effective against both radar dishes and AAA gun sites. This F-4G 'Wild Weasel' from the 563rd TFS *Aces* brandishes both a pair radar-homing AGM-45 Shrike missiles for stage one of the attack and a quartet of CBU-58/Bs to finish the job. The CBUs can be equipped with a mixture of impact- and delayed action-fused submunitions, highly effective at keeping 'heads down'. (DoD)

► An F-16C from the 363rd TFW based at Al Dhafra, United Arab Emirates, en route to its target with a mix of 'Winders, centreline 'long' AN/ALQ-119(V)-17 ECM pod, underwing drop tanks and, the main object of this study, its pair of CBU-87 Combined Effects Munitions. (DoD)

warhead forms a shaped charge to poke through the thick metal. The CBU-87 contains 214 BLU-97/B CEM submunitions while the CBU-89 uses a mix of 72 BLU-91/Bs and 24 BLU-92/Bs — larger, better-designed variations of the SUU-30 and Mk. 7 TMD which can be released from altitudes as diverse as tree-top level and 40,000ft. More significantly, the SUU-65 TMD features 'pop-out' tail surfaces designed to spin the dispenser at up to 2,500rpm for an optimum spread of submunitions — particularly useful when delivered from low level. This overcomes the tendency of the bomblets to scatter in a 'doughnut' pattern, as so many Vietnam-era cluster submunitions did. 'We would drop two or more CBUs in level flight', recollected former US Navy VA-196 *Main Battery* crewman Phil Waters, 'so that the donuts formed a long oval pattern. When dropped at night, they appeared as hundreds of tiny twinkles as each bomblet detonated, starting at a point and progressing along the flight path forming their donuts'. The newer CBUs are infinitely more flexible, and such 'canned' delivery tactics are no longer necessary, as was ably demonstrated in combat by the eighteen American F-111E fighter-bombers assigned to Incirlik in Turkey, which relied heavily on the new devices and dropped them, 'tossed' them and performed all manner of other deliveries to spread them over the target. Other key users included the long-legged B-52Gs operating from Diego

PRINCIPAL CLUSTER BOMB UNITS

Designation	Canister	Submunitions
Mk. 20 Rockeye Mod. 2	Mk. 7	247 M118 anti-tank
CBU-49B/B	SUU-30	217 BLU-61/B fragmentation
CBU-52B/B	SUU-30	254 BLU-61/B fragmentation
CBU-55A/B	SUU-49	3 BLU-73/B FAE
CBU-58B/B	SUU-30	650 BLU-63/B fragmentation
CBU-59/B	Mk. 7	717 BLU-77/B APAM
CBU-71A/B	SUU-30	650 BLU-68/B incendiary
CBU-72B/B	SUU-49 Mod.	3 BLU-73/B FAE
CBU-78/B Gator	Mk. 7	29 BLU-91/B anti-personnel mines / 38 BLU-92/B Gator anti-tank mines
CBU-87/B CEM	SUU-65	214 BLU-97/B CEM
CBU-89/B Gator	SUU-64	72 BLU-91/B anti-personnel mines / 24 BLU-92/B Gator anti-tank mines
CBU-97 SFW	SUU-64	10 BLU-108 'Skeet' anti-armour

Notes: APAM = Anti-*Matériel*, -Personnel. CEM = Combined Effects Munitions. FAE = Fuel-Air Explosive. SFW = autonomous Sensor-Fused Weapon.

◄ Britain's answer to the American CBU is the Hunting Engineering BL755 low-level cluster bomb, first used in combat during the Falklands Campaign in 1982. It remains highly effective. However, owing to the medium- to high-altitude tactics employed from early on in the Gulf War, only eight BL755s were dropped. The BDN-63 training rounds shown strapped to a Harrier in this photograph are black and white; live rounds are glossy green with a metallic rear section, with four complete white cradle bands and a yellow-for-live band at the front of the cylinder. (Tim Perry)

Garcia and Saudi Arabia. The venerable 'Buffs' carried a formidable load of up to three dozen apiece, sowing mines or destroying armour and POL storage facilities on tracts of land half a mile long! CEM 'carpet bombing' of the convoys retreating along the main highway out of Kuwait City towards Basra was one of the last actions planned, but this was ditched on humanitarian grounds as the Iraqi forces tucked tails and fled home.

Britain and France have developed their own highly effective 'sprinklers', the Hunting Engineering BL755 and the Thomson Brandt Armaments BLG-66 Belouga respectively, but as these are designed for high-speed, low-level delivery (their envisaged role in a European conflict), RAF and *Armée de l'Air* fighter-bombers committed to medium-altitude combat in the Gulf soon relinquished them in favour of the American CBUs, which can be dropped from higher altitudes, beyond the reach of small-arms fire. The dozen RAF Jaguar GR.1/1As deployed from Coltishall to Muharraq in Bahrain, for example, dropped only eight BL755s—but lobbed 385 CBU-87/B CEMs to add to the 750 1,000-pounders and 608 CRV-7 rockets expended over the course of 586 strike sorties.

Yet more sinister are the CBU-55 and -72, based on the SUU-49 TMD (see accompanying table) but packing ethylene oxide fuel-air explosives (FAE) which vaporize into a cloud and are set off by bursters fired into it at the appropriate moment: up to three large BLU-73/B FAE submunitions can be housed in the top-of-the-line model, to combine blast (at approximately 10 atmospheres' pressure) and fire to destroy surface targets. They have been likened to 'mini nuclear bombs', but with the supreme advantage that there are no deleterious after-effects from radiation—in other words, they are non-persistent. The results are better left to the imagination, as are those from the other all-up 'Bloo' weapons, which crash on impact to erupt in a sheet of suffocating flame (Napalm B) or to dispense lethal non-persistent gas, chemical or nerve agents. None of the latter 'mixes' has been assigned to active units, while the stocks of related chemicals are being gradually destroyed. Napalm, however, has been in regular use since the war in Korea. The chief fire-bombers during 'Desert Storm' were the US Marine Corps AV-8B Harrier close air supporters, which clocked up 3,380 sorties in all. Customary Harrier 'hang-ons' comprised four Mk. 7 TDMs, Mk. 77 napalm canisters or CBU-55/72 FAEs, which cleared swathes through the forward-entrenched Iraqi positions and effectively neutralized the oil-filled trenches which the enemy had so painstakingly laid out in an effort to hamper the advance of Coalition land forces.

Throughout the Gulf War, allied interdictors were targeted against airfields in an effort to keep the Iraqi Air Force securely on the

ground. It was all part of the superbly co-ordinated aerial jigsaw. Area coverage was again desirable to render the runways unserviceable, but CBUs were not the munitions for the task. In this instance, as Capt. Greg Lowrimore pointed out to the author a few years ago, you need something that can actually tear their strips apart: 'Realistically, you can go and spread stuff like the CBUs and it will take a little while to clean it up, but a couple of bulldozers later they're set to go. But if you tear up their runway they just have to sit there and figure out what they're going to do next—it's hard taking off with holes all over the place!'. This general requirement has spawned the development of rocket-powered, boosted kinetic munitions (BKM), among them the Matra BLU-107/B Durandal, and a wide variety of BKM or hollow-charged freefall munitions which are ejected from dispensers which remain attached to the aircraft (albeit jettisoned as soon as the munitions are dispensed).[7] In the Gulf, the stage was set to use one of the latest: Tornado with JP233. These missions demanded the coolest of nerves and took their toll of aircraft (though, in contradiction to erroneous contemporary speculation by the popular press, only one of the six Tornados lost to hostile fire was actually carrying the system when downed).

The Hunting Engineering JP233 is equally efficient at rendering docks, marshalling areas and other tough but sprawling targets inactive. Measuring some $21\frac{1}{2}$ft long and fitted to the Tornado's belly in pairs, the configuration has on occasion caused more than one pilot to remark 'It's tough to tell who's flying who!'. The system can be outfitted with a number of NATO-standard submunitions (compatible with the similar MBB MW-1 of German origin), and in RAF service these comprise thirty 57lb, SG357 runway-busting concrete-penetrators, together with no fewer than 215 $5\frac{1}{2}$lb HB876 area-denial (repair hindering) submunitions, contained in two bolt-on sections. The three squadrons which formed a total authorized unit establishment of 45 'Desert Pink' Tornado GR.1s assigned to Muharraq, Bahrain (home of 'Snoopy' and 'Triffid Airways'), plus Dhahran (the 'Palm Tree' unit) and Tabuk (the sharkmouthed aircraft) in Saudi Arabia, accounted for 100 JP233s expended in the first days of the war alone, with decisive results. Among their targets were the heavily defended Ubaydah bin al Jarrah, Al Asad and Al Taqaddum fields. 'Stormin'' H. Norman Schwarzkopf, the jovial Coalition C-in-C, described their role as 'absolutely superb. I'm damn' glad they are with us', countering some ill-timed criticisms from Chief of Staff Gen. Colin Powell. Indeed, with the right crews at the helm, JP233 established its worth, and work is now underway further to improve the penetrating capability of the warheads. It was

► Matra's BLU-107/B Durandal has proved to be a cost-effective runway-busting weapon. The USAF acquired 5,000 of these 'one shot, one hole' devices for use on its F-111E/F 'Varks', which may carry up to a dozen at a time. *L'Armée de l'Air* Mirage 2000s customarily carry up to eight, four on the centreline and four more on the adjacent ventral fuselage rails. (Peter E. Davies)

▼ RAF ground crews wheel a Hunting Engineering JP233 runway-busting dispenser under the belly of a Tornado GR.1. About 100 JP233 munitions were expended early on in the Gulf War during the hazardous strikes on Iraqi airfields. (Royal Air Force)

intended originally that JP233 equip the USAF F-111 force also, but the Americans are now setting their sights slightly higher and are developing winged, rocket-powered and glide bulk munitions dispensers which possess both long-range stand-off delivery and stealth features, under the TSSAM (Tri-Service Standoff Attack Missile) effort and Project 'Have Slick'.[8]

'SMART' BOMBS

The most successful of all bombs used during the fierce air war over Baghdad and the outlying industrial centres and air bases were the so-called 'smart' bombs, known to those who used them by the official acronym PGMs, standing for Precision Guided Munitions. Introduced to combat in South-East Asia in May 1967 in their early, experimental form, and famous for their 'bridge busting' exploits during the 'Linebacker' offensives of 1972, the weapons come from the manufacturers in boxed format for easy storage (known as 'groups') and can be simply unpacked, checked-out by a test trolley and then 'plugged' on to the existing range of 'iron' bombs by means of bolt-on collars. They transform the humble 'dumb' munition, which is subject merely to the laws of gravity, into a glide weapon which can partially defy natural ballistics to home in on a target with a CEP (Circular Error Probable) measured in inches. This degree of accuracy is needed for a number of reasons: first, with on-the-spot

media coverage of many a target, it is necessary, for political as well as humanitarian reasons, to avoid civilian casualties (euphemistically known as 'collateral damage'). Second, although these weapons fetch an all-up price of between $12,000 and $150,000, depending on their mark, it is far more cost-effective to hit a key target with a handful of bombs than to commit entire formations of multi-million-dollar fighter-bombers and their crews to the mêlée without any guarantee of success.

One of the chief categories of 'smart' weapons comprises the electro-optically guided bombs (EOGB) family. These are locked on to a target by means of a daylight TV or night-time imaging infra-red sensor in the nose of the weapon, which relays a bomb's-eye-view picture to the cockpit. The pilot (or, more usually, his back- or right-seat navigator or 'Wizzo') then acquires the target image and locks the chosen impact point under the crosshairs. Lock-on can be accomplished prior to weapons release (LOBL) for a launch-and-leave attack, or after launch (LOAL, which 99 out of 100 times means guiding the bomb all the way to target) when an active data link is present to transmit the bomb's TV imagery back into the cockpit and the fine-tuning of the crosshair position back to the bomb. The first of the breed was the purpose-built (not bomb-adapted) Martin Marietta AGM-62 Walleye, introduced to combat by A-4 'Scooters' of

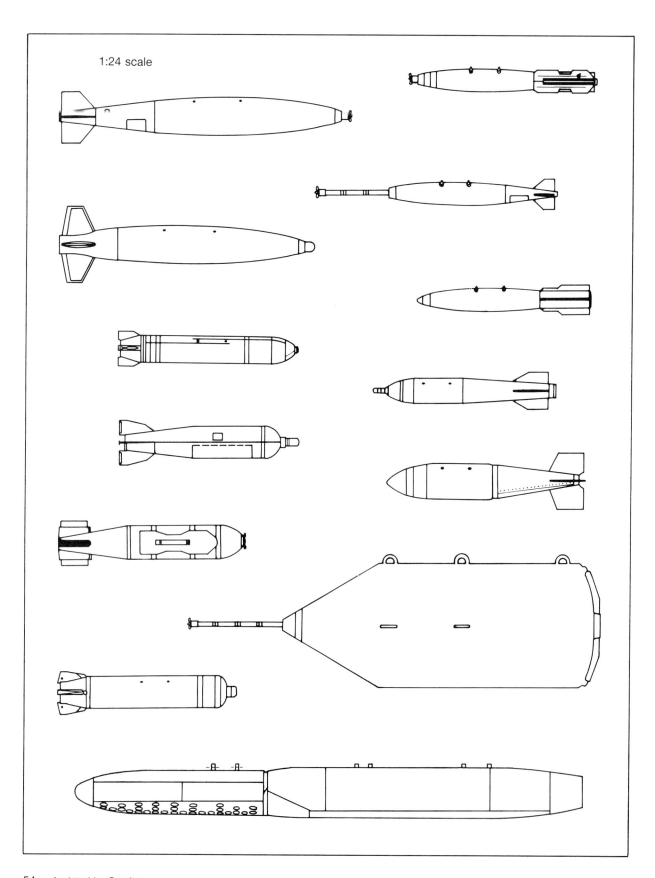

1:24 scale

◄ 'Iron' bombs and cluster munitions. Left, top to bottom: Mk. 84, 2,000lb LDGP bomb; Mk. 84 AIR; Mk. 7 cluster bomb canister; SUU-30/B cluster bomb canister; BL-755 British cluster bomb dispenser (top view); and SUU-64/B, –65/B Tactical Munitions Dispensers. Right, top to bottom: Mk. 82 Snakeye 500lb retarded bomb (or externally identical Mk. 36 DST); Mk. 82 LDGP bomb with 36in 'Daisy Cutter' fitted; Mk. 82 AIR; French Matra 250kg 'iron' bomb; British 1,000lb 'iron' bomb; BLU-82/B HCLC 'Mother of Bombs' with 48in 'Daisy Cutter' and parachute pack fitted; and JP233 munitions-dispensing unit. (Author)

▶ The Martin Marietta AGM-62 Walleye TV-guided glide bomb was introduced to combat by the US Navy on 11 March 1967, by Cdr. Homer Smith, VA-212 skipper. Twenty-four years later it was still going strong, as evidenced by this 'SLUF' from VA-72 Blue Hawks, just about to 'cat' with a Walleye from the deck of the USS John F. Kennedy during the height of Operation 'Desert Storm'. Stand-off communication was conducted by means of the AN/AWW-9 data link pod. Altogether 124 of the ER/DL Walleye 2 (Mk. 13, Mod. 0) were expended during the six-week aerial campaign. (DoD)

▶ From the outset, the USAF adopted a modular approach to 'smart' bombs by creating kits which could be fitted to the standard range of 'iron' bombs. One of the pioneers was the Rockwell International GBU-8 Hobos EOGB-1 (Electro-Optically Guided Bomb, Mk. 1), adapted from the Mk. 84. A GBU-9 version, based on the M118 3,000lb HCLC munition, also existed. Hobos was used for first time in May 1972, with mixed results. (Rockwell International)

the Seventh Fleet. The first strike was undertaken by Cdr. Homer Smith on 11 March 1967. Flying from the deck of the USS *Bon Homme Richard* in company with four Phantoms which provided TARCAP, he released his glide bomb against the Sam Son barracks and watched it enter through a window and demolish the building with its 1,000lb warhead. Successive attacks produced equal results against the Phu Dien Chau and the Thanh Hoa 'Dragon's Jaw' bridges, with virtually every Walleye gliding to target as advertised—65 out of 68 dropped by 'Bonnie Dick's' jets during the seven-month WESTPAC cruise. Navy A-4s, A-6s and A-7s were all subsequently outfitted for the weapon. Until very recently, Walleye remained the most successful EOGB and was acquired in limited numbers by the US and Israeli Air Forces. By 1972 it had been adapted to the larger-yield 'Fat Albert' configuration, linked to a jam-resistant AN/AWW-9 data-link pod

for LOAL (known as Extended Range/Data-Link, or simply ER/DL), especially useful for 'buddy smart bombing', when one aircraft lobbed the bomb, leaving a companion at a relatively safe distance away from the target to acquire it and ensure that the weapon was guided to the desired impact point (after which time the two aircraft were free to trade roles and 'work' another target). While it enjoyed its greatest success in Vietnam, it was also usefully employed by the US Navy's A-7E 'SLUFs' flying from the Red Sea, on their final cruise aboard the USS *John F. Kennedy* when the Gulf Crisis broke out. Alongside A-6Es, VA-46 *Clansmen* and VA-72 *Blue Hawks*, in a timely and effective manner, helped to run down the inventory of Walleyes accounting for 124 drops, before heading for home and retirement—though, with typical American bravado, one of the aircraft (minus its stores) was towed through New York's main avenues during the ensuing ticker-tape celebrations!

A much more sophisticated and powerful weapon, but one which has had a considerably longer gestation period, is the USAF equivalent built by Rockwell International. In its comparatively crude, Vietnam-era format it was known as the GBU-8 Hobos (homing bomb system) and was fitted to one-ton Mk. 84 'hammers' and M118, 3,000lb general-purpose munitions. It met with mixed success during its introduction to combat on 10 May 1972, when seven of the weapons broke lock with their assigned target, the seemingly indestructible Paul Doumer bridge, and

careered away to cause relatively little damage. The chief problem was that attack headings and times had to be precise so that the weapon's narrow field-of-view (FOV) sensor could hold its lock on to the desired 'contrast point'. A change in the shadows (such as that caused by the sun moving in and out of cloud) would cause the bomb to go 'dumb' and miss its target by a wide berth. To a certain extent, the US Navy were more adept at EOGB mission-planning, and it took the Air Force several months to learn, by trial and error, how to use the new weapons. The technology, moreover, was not yet sufficiently mature: it is also all too easy to overlook the fact that Vietnam was the great proving ground for experimental devices, many of which went awry.

In a great postwar initiative spawned by the Pave Strike project, Rockwell pooled 'sensor' knowledge with Hughes Missiles (who were in the process of developing a TV-guided missile, the Maverick), and created the GBU-15 as a successor to Hobos, again based on the Mk. 84.[9] This went into production in 1977 for the Israeli Air Force and still forms one of the chief 'smart' weapons of that Service. The USAF continued to tinker with the design for a further five years before it finally entered operational service with the F-4E Phantoms of the 4th TFW at Seymour-Johnson, North Carolina, and the 52nd TFW *Fightin' Fifty-Second* at Spangdahlem, Germany. TSgt. Fox was at Nellis Tactical Fighter Weapons Center when the *Fourth-but-First* conducted the earliest Red Flag wargames

▼ The spectacular Rockwell GBU-15 EOGB-2 was developed in the 1970s as a worthy successor to Hobos, using advanced TV or imaging infra-red guidance. It is capable of being 'tossed' at low level at supersonic speeds, at ranges of up to eight miles from the target. High-altitude launches furnish a range of over twenty miles. Stand-off communication, via radio/radar data link, is furnished by the Hughes AN/AXQ-14 pod, which relays TV pictures back to the launch aircraft or to a 'buddy' and conveys course correction commands to the bomb, which is 'flown' all the way to the target. Here a GBU-15(V)-1/B is let loose from a Phantom from the 3rd TFS *Peugeots*. (Rockwell International)

▶ A total of seventy $150,000 infra-red-guided GBU-15(V)-1/Bs were dropped by the F-111Fs of the 48th TFW(P), flying from Taif in Saudi Arabia against fixed targets in Iraq and Kuwait, including the oil manifolds the Iraqis were using to create huge oil slicks in the Persian Gulf. These stopped the spills at their source. A nuclear version of the GBU-15, equipped with the Tomahawk's W80 warhead, was abandoned in FY 80. (USAFE)

with the weapon: 'They dropped two from the same aircraft and they were both on target. One went right into an eight-foot hole and the other hit the side and went in!' By the time hostilities had broken out in the Gulf, the chief exponents were the 493rd TFS *Roos-*

ters based in Taif, Saudi Arabia, flying F-111Fs as the 'Freedom Squadron'. A number of its crews had perfected their use of the system after years of dedicated training, and it paid off. As one former 493rd TFS aviator noted, 'Virtually the only time during "Desert

►As well as having two forms of guidance based on the E-O devices developed for the Maverick missile, the EOGB-2 is also available in two formats when mated to the Mk. 84 'hammer': the GBU-15(V)-1/B, equipped with wide-chord MXU-724 aerofoils; and, as depicted here strapped to an Eglin-based munitions development Phantom, the GBU-15(V)-2/B version with short-chord MXU-787 wings. The short-chord configuration is, however, now used chiefly with the GBU-15(V)-31/32 model fitted with the BLU-109/B penetrating warhead. (Rockwell International)

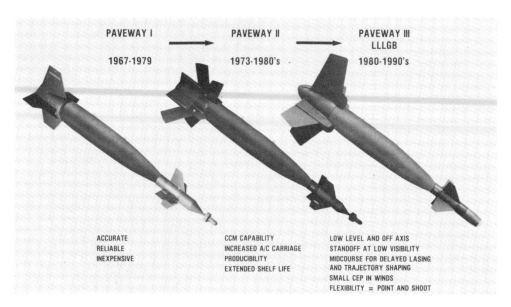

PAVEWAY I	PAVEWAY II	PAVEWAY III LLLGB
1967-1979	1973-1980's	1980-1990's

ACCURATE
RELIABLE
INEXPENSIVE

CCM CAPABILITY
INCREASED A/C CARRIAGE
PRODUCIBILITY
EXTENDED SHELF LIFE

LOW LEVEL AND OFF AXIS
STANDOFF AT LOW VISIBILITY
MIDCOURSE FOR DELAYED LASING
AND TRAJECTORY SHAPING
SMALL CEP IN WINDS
FLEXIBILITY = POINT AND SHOOT

◀ The evolution of the Texas Instruments 'Paveway' series, showing the principal differentiating features of the 2,000lb GBU-10/B, GBU-10C-E/B and GBU-24/B models. (Texas Instruments)

Storm'' the F-111F was singled out for special attention was when it used two GBU-15(V)-2/B stand-off weapons to destroy oil manifolds the Iraqis were using to create history's largest oil slick in the Persian Gulf.' This occurred on 28 January 1991 when Capt. Brad Seipel guided two of the glide bombs into the Almadi pumping stations in occupied Kuwait, cutting off the spill at its source. Some seventy GBU-15s were used in all, each of which could be 'tossed' at supersonic speeds for a glide range of 8–20 miles, subject to launch altitude. A two-way data link was furnished by the Hughes AN/AXQ-14 pod, bolted to the rear of the F-111s and permitting the 'Wizzos' to 'fly' the bombs all the way to target.

In its latest guise it is being refitted with short-chord cruciform wings, which the manufacturers claim are cheaper to produce. This new arrangement is used with the BLU-109/B destructor to create the GBU/15(V)-31/32 (the so-called GBU-15I) and was tested with 2,000lb category CBUs. The SUU-54 canister is still being actively considered for this role, to create a 'smart' radar-smasher for the defence-suppression forces.

The most famous (or infamous, depending on one's perspective) of the PGMs are the laser-guided bombs (LGBs), which have been an outstanding success ever since the first KMU-342, 750lb types were dropped by F-4Ds of the 8th TFW *Wolfpack* on POL and truck dumps dotted along the Ho Chi Minh Trail in Laos back in the winter of 1967. By 1972, when the air war over North Vietnam

was resumed in earnest, these had evolved into the Texas Instruments Paveway I family, designed to fit the M118 and Mk. 80 series LDGP 'iron' bombs in 'high' and 'low' speed format. Between May and December that year they helped to demolish over 106 bridges, along with other pinpoint targets such as power-generating plants, docks and Radio Hanoi—most of which were hitherto off-limits because of the fear of excessive collateral damage—coercing the North Vietnamese back to the peace conference table in Paris. The family was superseded by the longer-glide-range, tri-service Paveway II series by 1980, and more recently by the Paveway III low-level LGB format which can be 'tossed' at low level by virtue of its solid-state proportional guidance, which replaced the old electro-mechanical 'bang-bang'

▼ A sharkmouthed Paveway II GBU-10 being eased on to the pylon of a sharkmouthed Phantom—all part of a normal day's work for the 3rd TFW, which until the early spring of 1991 had its headquarters at Clark Field in the Philippines. The nose seeker section has yet to be fitted to the weapon. (PACAF)

► Capt. Wylie E. Lovelady, from the F-111F-equipped 494th *Liberty* squadron, checks out the nose seeker of a Paveway GBU-10E/B as part of the customary 'pre-flight walkaround' preparatory to a strike mission from Taif, Saudi Arabia. (TSgt. Rose S. Reynolds/USAF)

system, overcoming earlier problems of weapons running out of kinetic energy, short of the target, particularly if designation commenced too early. British CPU-123/B equivalents, licence-manufactured by Portsmouth Aviation, have been adapted for the domestically manufactured 'racing green' 1,000-pounder, while France's Matra company has evolved its own breed. Both these European systems work on principles identical to those of the American Paveway II.

Unlike the EOGBs, however, the LGBs are not launch-and-leave weapons: instead, the chosen aim-point (the 'spot') is marked with an invisible beam of coded laser energy from a suitable designator. The bomb, whose steering vanes are coupled to the gimballed or electronic laser seeker, then 'flies' into the reflected 'laser basket', right to the 'spot'.

► Low-level 'Toss' bombing of the GBU-15 glide bomb, at a range of up to eight miles from the target. Similar tactics are used to lob cluster bombs 2–3 miles from the aimpoint.

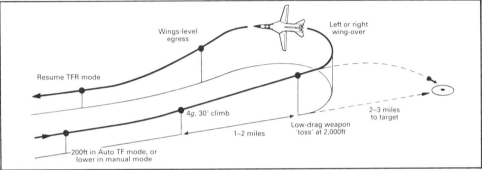

► Direct 'solo' and indirect 'buddy' attack tactics which may be used with the GBU-15 glide bomb and AN/AXQ-14 data link system. The US Navy uses a similar approach with the AN/AWW-9 pod and AGM-62 ER/DL Walleye or SLAM, which are typically flown all the way to target.

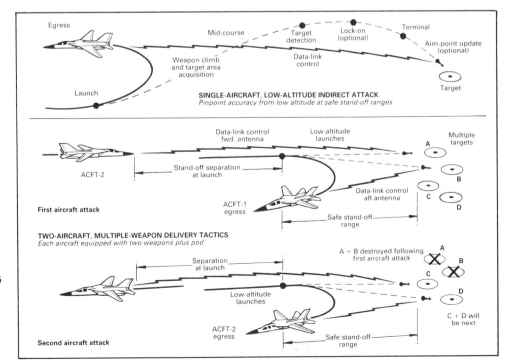

Designation in turn can be provided by ground forces; or, when on interdiction missions deep in enemy territory, by the attacking aircraft or a 'buddy', using a laser gun and receiver boresighted with a TV or FLIR (forward-looking infra-red) camera, so that the air crewmen (again, typically a 'Wizzo') can acquire the target on a TV display in the cockpit, centre the target under the cross-hairs and 'squirt' the laser gun on to the precise aiming point for the bombs to home in on. 'Buddy-bombing' and 'buddy-lasing' were a last resort, used by both the British Tornado and Buccaneer and American F-15E outfits during the height of 'Desert Storm', while the preferred tactic is always self-designation—known as 'autonomous bombing'. 'Desert Storm' witnessed the utilization of the whole range of related laser 'guns', including Pave Spike, Pave Tack, LANTIRN, TRAM, ATLIS and TIALD.[10] The most highly touted laser bombers of the conflict were the forty-four F-117As, which were based at Khamis Mushayt (known as 'Tonopah East') in south-west Saudi Arabia under the command of Col. Al Whitley. Crews riding the tip of the arrowhead-shaped, butterfly-tailed machines opened up the night attacks in the harrowing early hours of 17 January 1991 using their one-man, largely automatic IRADS (infra-red attack and designator system) to guide the 'bunker-busting' BLU-109/B-equipped models of the Paveway LGB—the GBU-10G-H-J (GBU-10I) and

◄ Solid-seeker 'Groups' were introduced on the Paveway III LLLGB (low-level laser-guided bomb), which is equally effective when dropped from altitude. The weapon is the speciality of the USAF F-111F force; when fitted with a Paveway II tail and a BLU-109/B warhead, it also becomes the GBU-27A/B, the main LGB armament for the Lockheed F-117A stealth fighter. (Peter E. Davies)

◄ Paveway LGBs were used with considerable success in the Gulf to 'plink' individual tanks and hardened aircraft shelters using multiple aircraft 'Wagon Wheel' attack tactics, as these two photographs show. The F-111Fs alone used 500 GBU-10E/Bs, 400 GBU-10Is 150 GBU-24/Bs and nearly 1,000 GBU-24A/Bs, accounting for two-thirds of all PGMs dropped by the USAF. (DoD)

▼ This magnificent wide-angle photograph shows an F-117A from the 37th TFW *Defenders of the Crossroads* safely tucked away in its luxurious subterranean hangar at Khamis Mushayt ('Tonopah East'), in Saudi Arabia. Dangling from the retractable weapons racks are a pair of GBU-10G-J/B (the so-called GBU-10I) bombs. The 'Bat Planes' each can carry two of either the GBU-10E/B (Paveway II plus Mk. 84 warhead), GBU-10G-J (P-II plus BLU-109/B), GBU-27/B (P-III nose, P-II tail plus Mk. 84) or GBU-27A/B (P-III nose, P-II tail plus BLU-109/B) configured LGBs—basically, all pinpoint one-ton laser bombs. (DoD)

-27A/B—with 'surgical precision'. In all, the unit's two operational squadrons and contingent of experienced instructors from the *Nightstalkers*, *Ghost Riders* and *Bandits* flew 1,271 combat sorties without loss, during which time they dropped over 2,000 tons of LGBs for a 95 per cent success rate. Only slight modifications were required to accommodate the standard 'smart' bombs in the 'Bat Plane's' weapons bay, including slightly shorter attachment collars and clipped steering fins, as well as the Paveway II class tail which offered a steeper bomb trajectory to assist with BLU-109/B penetration.

To a certain extent, the deeds of the F-117As tended to eclipse the equally dramatic exploits of the other 'plinkers', the gaggles of Buccaneers, Tornados and F-111Fs actively engaged in knocking out tanks, HASs and LOCs. The statistics speak loudly of the 'smart' bombs' staggering success: excluding the 'smart' TV-guided missiles (dealt with later), of the 7,400 tons of PGMs dropped by the Americans, 90 per cent were handled by the USAF of which no less than 61 per cent were deposited by the often-neglected F-111Fs! PGMs provided an overall 80–90 per cent success rate. In marked contrast, as one USAF officer explained, 'dumb' bombs 'only hit their targets about 5–25 per cent of the time, depending on the target type. It probably cost less than $200 million in PGMs to put Iraq back into the pre-industrial age'. Mostly, the 81,000 tons of 'dumb' bombs

dropped merely served to harass enemy ground formations by day between the pinpoint attacks conducted under the cloak of darkness. F-16s, for example, would roll in in flights of four at a time (!), each to lob a quartet of Mk. 84 'hammers' on a hit-or-miss basis. These tactics merely served to accelerate the fatigue cracks that began to appear on the 'Lawn Darts' (as the F-16s are sometimes irreverently referred to), without adding a great deal to the bombing effort, and five of them were brought down by hostile fire. No fewer than 790 of the early-build aircraft may soon be winging their way to the scrap heap, long before the 15–20-year-old F-111Fs follow suit.

'DEEP THROAT'

Indeed, it was the 'smart' bombers, and Col. Tom Lennon's sixty-six F-111Fs based at Taif in particular, which played the biggest role in the air strikes: 'Like the proverbial "bad girls", they went everywhere—including Baghdad—to destroy bridges, airfields, tanks, artillery, pumping stations, communications facilities and anything else that would hold still long enough to have a [smart] bomb put on it. Behind closed doors, one very senior commander said, "I want this target hit—give it to the F-111s"!' The aircraft lived up to their reputation of being 'smart bombers *and* smart airplanes'. The final tally of 2,203 targets obliterated by the four 48th TFW *Liberty Wing* squadrons (the 492nd TFS

▲ Nicknamed 'The Ghost of Baghdad', Lockheed's radical polyhedron stealth fighter flew 1,271 combat sorties while in the Persian Gulf, carrying all its ordnance internally. Its clean skin and unique aerodynamics demand touch-down speeds at 165kt—hence the large ring-slot drag 'chute. Fifty-six of these aircraft were in service at the time of writing. (Charles T. Robbins)

Justice, 493rd *Freedom*, 494th *Liberty* and 495th *Indy*) included direct hits on at least 920 tanks, 252 artillery pieces, 245 HASs, thirteen runways and a dozen bridges, with only superficial damage to two aircraft. They also made their mark in other ways. The Defense Support Program missile warning satellite was abruptly woken by the largest non-nuclear explosion ever created when the leader at the apex of a twenty-ship 'Vark' formation arrived at Tallil airfield in south-west Iraq: 'As a result of his direct hit on an ammunition storage area, smoke rose to 30,000ft and only one other aircraft in the attack was able to [see though the quagmire to] deliver its weapons'! The unit's *pièce dc résistance* came on the final night of the war, on 27 February, when Project 'Deep Throat', the 'ultimate LGB', was deployed in combat.

The background story to 'Deep Throat' bears telling, as it represents one of the most rapid weapons developments in the annals of modern air warfare. In December 1990, engineers at Eglin AFB, Florida, were told they had ten weeks to develop and field the weapon (a process which customarily takes 3½ years!), after a Lockheed engineer hit upon the idea of encasing explosives in lengths of used, off-the-shelf barrels from US Army self-propelled howitzers. According to the Project Manager, Maj. Dick Wright, the effort 'acquired added urgency . . . when members of the Air Staff at the Pentagon saw a graphic [diagram] illustrating the shortcomings of existing 500- and 2,000-pound bombs

against hardened bunkers in the newspaper *USA Today*. It showed that none would get to the target, and that was pretty accurate!'. Technicians began to cut, remachine and bore out an extra two inches from thirty of the gun barrels at the Army's Watervliet Arsenal in New York on 25 January and airfreighted them to Eglin 22 days later, where they were stood in the ground and filled with molten Tritonal explosives by a 'bucket brigade'. The bombs were then mated to a modified GBU-27 guidance kit, to create the 4,700lb GBU-28. During subsequent tests, the first from an F-111F on the morning of 24 February at Tonopah Test Range, Nevada, the bomb hit the target and penetrated deeper than 100ft! On the afternoon of the 26th, a second weapon was fitted to a sled at Holloman AFB,

UNDERWATER MINES

Mine	Warhead	Weight (lb)	Fin kit	Fusing/depth
Mk. 36 DST	Mk. 82	560	Mk. 15	Time-delay
Mk. 40 DST	Mk. 83	1,060	MAU-91	Time-delay
Mk. 41 DST	Mk. 84	2,000	Unknown	Time-delay
Mk. 55 Mod.2		2,160	n/a	Magnetic, 600ft
Mod. 3		2,180	n/a	Pressure/magnetic, 150ft
Mod. 5		2,180	n/a	Acoustic/magnetic, 150ft
Mod. 6		2,190	n/a	Pressure/acoustic/magnetic, 150ft
Mod. 7		2,190	n/a	Dual-channel magnetic, 600ft
Mk. 56 OA 05		2,150	n/a	Dual-channel magnetic, 1,200ft
OA 06		2,215	n/a	As OA 05, with faired nose
Mk. 60	Mk. 46	2,360	n/a	Captor anti-submarine torpedo
Mk. 62	Mk. 82	580	Mk. 15	Quickstrike, easy-to-assemble influence-fused, 300ft
Mk. 63 Mod. 0	Mk. 83	1,020	EX 9	Quickstrike, easy-to-assemble influence-fused, 300ft
Mod. 1	Mk. 83	1,080	EX 126/9	Quickstrike, easy-to-assemble influence-fused, 300ft
Mk. 64 OA 1/2	Mk. 84	2,130	EX 127/9	Quickstrike, easy-to-assemble influence-fused, 300ft
OA 3	Mk. 84	2,145	EX 128/9	Quickstrike, easy-to-assemble influence-fused, 300ft
Mk. 65		2,360	EX 7	Quickstrike, easy-to-assemble influence-fused, 300ft

Notes: Most of the warheads are based on the standard Mk. 80 series to create DST 'Destructors', the remainder comprising: Mk. 55 & 'Quickstrike' 'Bottom Mines', Mk. 56 'Moored Mines', and the Mk. 60 Captor (encapsulated torpedo). The whole range are used by US Navy carrier-going aircraft, and select USAF B-52Gs and NATO air arms.

New Mexico, and punched through 22ft of reinforced concrete slabs before shooting a further half mile downrange! The pace continued. That same morning a pair of the weapons, still warm to the touch from the cooling Tritonal, were loaded aboard a C-141B Starlifter and ferried to Taif in Saudi. Within 5½ hours of arrival they were strapped to a pair of 492nd TFS *Justice* 'Varks', bound for Iraq.

Lt. Col. Dave White and his 'Wizzo', Capt. Tom Himes, in the 'slot' position of the two-ship flight led by Lt. Col. Ken Combs and his navigator, Maj. Jerry Hust, dropped their penetrator on to a command and control bunker at Al Taji airfield, just north of Baghdad. 'It was an unknown munition. We didn't have any delivery parameters and didn't know any of its characteristics', recalled the crewmen, so 'the profile we flew was pretty much what we'd been flying all along'—except that to impart extra kinetic energy the crew executed a step-climb to higher than normal LGB release altitudes. 'What we were aiming for was basically a piece of dirt', recalled Maj. Hust, beneath which sat the enemy bunker. The effect may have been decisive. As another USAF officer noted, 'Much like the atomic bombs which ended World War II, these bombs sent a clear message to the Iraqi leadership that they were personally at risk—in a matter of hours they accepted all United Nations resolutions'! The balance of 26 bombs remain on standby while series development and manufacture of purpose-built equivalents, the I-1000/2000/4000 'family', is one of the United States' current priority bomb programmes. Today's freefall munitions are making very different holes indeed.

NOTES TO CHAPTER TWO

1. Low-drag bombs were pioneered in the 1930s but fell out of favour with the introduction of the multi-engined 'heavies' which could employ hefty loads of HCLC munitions, including incendiaries, internally. However, as late as the mid-1960s, aircraft were sometimes obliged to tote vintage, drag-inducing, box-finned ordnance, known as 'fat' bombs. This was particularly true of US Marine Corps aircraft ground-based in South Vietnam and Thailand. Their use has also been accredited to the so-called 'bomb shortages' of 1965–67 at the height of the 'Rolling Thunder' campaign against North Vietnam, a situation which was alleviated only by a massive increase in production of the Mk. 80 series and the introduction of the first cost-effective 'smart' bombs, described below.
2. Among them the widely-used D704 'buddy' refuelling pod, lightweight nuclear weapons and their BDU (Bomb, Dummy Unit) training equivalents and the first reliable triple and multiple ejection racks (TER and MER), which effectively increased bomb carriage capability by a factor of up to six.
3. Another mix of munitions which has a horrific effect, in this instance against enemy ground troops, is that of Snakeye and napalm, known to the aircrews as 'Snake and Nape' (= 'Shake and Bake', = 'Crispy Critters'!)
4. Refer to Chapter 3 for an examination of modern air-to-surface missiles and to Chapter 4 for a fuller description of the nuclear bombs. Stocks of American and British nuclear gravity bombs in Europe peaked between 1973 and 1982 at around 2,000 warheads, distributed mainly among the American F-111 and F-4 units and the RAF Vulcan and Buccaneer squadrons. By 1993, this number should have fallen to less than 700.
5. See 'Smart Bombs', below.
6. *Ibid*. See also 'Deep Throat', below.
7. Refer to Chapter 3.
8. *Ibid*.
9. *Ibid*.
10. Refer to Chapter 5. 'Buddy lasing' is complicated, difficult and 'spring-loaded to the disaster position [as a Tornado crew found out]. It's especially hard at night, except when it is extensively pre-briefed and pre-planned (e.g., when there are *not* enough pods to go around). A loss of a pod is more likely to result in mission abort than a "buddy lasing".'

◀ 'Who ya gonna call? HAS-Busters!'. 'Plinking' aircraft shelters was a mission performed with equal success by the RAF's Tornado establishment. The Paveway II CPU-123/B 1,000lb LGBs, carried in pairs or trios by the GR.1s, were guided to their targets by lasers 'squirted' by Pave Spike Buccaneers or TIALD Tornados. (Via Tim Perry)

3.
GOPHER-ZAPPERS

IT HAS BEEN estimated that throughout Operation 'Desert Storm', Coalition air arms were expending an average of £6 million worth of air-delivered munitions *an hour*. Accounting for a considerable percentage of this cost were the air-to-ground missiles (AGMs), by far the most expensive stores to be carried aloft during the relentless six-week aerial onslaught. Among the names bandied about during the press conferences were Hellfire and SLAM, a codename and an acronym for two of the West's most lethal conventional weapons.

MARTEL, MAVERICK AND POPEYE
Just too early to see action during Operation 'Desert Storm' was the pioneering Anglo-French Martel, the last of which were

expended during RAF exercises the previous autumn. It was for a long time the world's most accurate EO-guided missile, setting standards which everyone was obliged to follow. Developed by BAe Dynamics and SA Matra as a joint venture beginning in 1964 as two concurrent weapons systems—the AJ168 TV-guided model, and the AS37 anti-radar version (hence the name, an acronym for Missile Anti-Radar, Television)—the weapon offered a range of up to 35 miles when launched from altitude, using LOBL plus post-launch updates or straightforward LOAL techniques, by means of a GEC Sensors 'Data Pack' microwave link contained in a slim pod, similar to the Walleye/AWW-9 and GBU-15/AXQ-14 combinations described in the last chapter and using imagery

▼ A Royal Saudi Air Force Tornado on parade at Farnborough's 1986 SBAC exposition with the diverse stores available for combat operations, including an In Flight Systems 'buddy' aerial refuelling pod and Martel, Sky Flash, Sea Eagle and HARM missiles. (Author)

relayed from the missile's nose-mounted vidicon camera—but at least seven years ahead of the American competition, which was at the time struggling to produce an adequate seeker. GEC engineer Ian Hunter, who worked on the Martel, has pointed out that the first such microwave remote-control demonstrations were carried out as long ago as 1967. Developed originally for use from the TSR.2 and Vulcan, Martel passed to the Buccaneer S.2 when the RAF switched to low-level interdiction tactics, on which it entered operational service in 1970. (Nimrod maritime patrol aircraft were wired up for the system but never carried it.) Its accuracy was staggering. Crews chose their aimpoint, such as a window in a building or the soft spot in the flank of a ship using a new display in the navigator's 'office', locked the missile on to the target by means of a graticule (a grid as opposed to crosshairs) and set the missile on course, refining the aimpoint by means of a joystick tracking control and the microwave data link. Improvements to image quality came around 1978 after the package's electrical system had been fine-tuned (Mr. Hunter recalls sitting in the back of a Buccaneer which was plumbed into a power cart, to permit him to work out the 'bugs' at first hand). In all, five models were manufactured, excluding France's AS37 which was equip-

ped with an EMD AD37 passive radar-hunting device, all of them way ahead of their time.[1] Yet its astonished engineers had to suffer the ignominy of watching their work fade away into oblivion. Disinterest from the Ministry of Defence has been matched only by the RAF's penchant for pursuing off-the-shelf American weapons systems, such as the SLAM (described below), effectively squandering the firm lead established by Martel.

Of all the American missiles launched in the Gulf War, perhaps the best-known is the Hughes AGM-65 Maverick, designed around a 1ft-diameter, scaled-up Falcon airframe, capped with a LOBL seeker head, propelled by a Thiokol boost-sustain TX-481 (or the follow-on, reduced-smoke TX-633) solid rocket motor and steered by a set of small cruciform tailfins. Maximum aerodynamic range is stated to be 12.5 nautical miles, though in practice it is something less than two-thirds of that, subject to launch altitude. Fielded experimentally during the 'Linebacker' offensives against North Vietnam in 1972, where approximately thirty trials rounds were expended, and introduced officially into squadron service with the F-4E Phantoms of the 334th TFS *Eagles* on 22 June the following year, Maverick gave the USAF its long sought-after air-to-surface fire-and-forget

▼ The key subject here is Grumman's mock-up of its A2F Intruder, but the items of particular interest include the AGM-12 Bullpup optically guided missile and the belly-mounted ASM-N-8 Corvus which was to be fitted with a W40 nuclear warhead. These devices were 'state-of-the-art' in 1961, when missile technology was flourishing. (Grumman Archives)

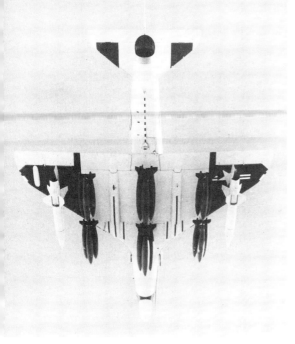

guided missile capability. Expended in quantity by the *Chey'l Ha'Avir* that autumn immediately following its hasty introduction during the 'Nickel Glass' emergency resupply effort, the weapon demonstrated a 'kill' rate in excess of 82 per cent, with crews whose 'hands-on' training, owing to the exigencies of the Yom Kippur conflict, consisted solely of taking off with the freshly unpacked missiles and firing them at Arab armour 'off the bat'! Maverick's daytime TV seeker worked flawlessly in the idyllically clear desert skies. However, its performance amidst the grey clouds of North-West Europe and the muggy

interior of the Far East, where Maverick was being issued in quantity to front-line USAF Phantom units, was not so exciting. The chief problem was the 'Alpha's' relatively wide, 5°-FOV ooolior, which often forced pilots to press their attack runs well within rocket motor range in order to ensure an adequate TV lock; or, alternatively, to spend excessive time in vulnerable, jink-free, steady flight. At this stage in NATO's turbulent history the knock-on effects of Yom Kippur and the threat of the ever-malevolent 'Bear's' armour were running amok within the closed corridors of the Pentagon, and of the Office of the DDRE (Defense Directorate of Research & Engineering) in particular. The fighter pilots' moans were answered quickly by the introduction of the ostensibly identical AGM-65B in May 1975, fitted with a now standard DSU-27/B 2.5°-FOV weapons seeker which effectively quadrupled the size of the target image in the display. Lock-on times in the rear 'office' (which varied with crew co-ordination skills) tended to fall by half, and were reduced further when Hughes introduced the 'Quick Draw' capability: Mavericks were typically carried in twos or threes at a time on LAU-88A missile racks, and 'Quick Draw' permitted one missile to be boresighted with the lock-on of another, making minor slews to place its crosshairs on a nearby second or third target a speedy process. Production of both TV-guided models closed at 30,000 rounds, including exports to seventeen overseas customers. Its seekers,

◄A pretty, red and white A-4 'Scooter' assigned to the Naval Ordnance Test Station shows off its armoury of Mk. 82 and Mk. 83 LDGP 'slicks' and an outboard load of ASM N-7, AGM-12A/B Bullpup missiles. Bullpups were guided to target via radio control, the pilot following the missile flare, in his gunsight, right through to impact. Developed for the US Navy, the missile featured a 250lb warhead (enlarged to 1,000lb with the AGM-12C Bullpup B of 1962) and a speed of Mach 1.8, and was used in limited numbers also by the USAF's F-105D and F-4C forces in SE Asia. (Douglas Aircraft)

▼ After some clandestine experimental test-shots in South-East Asia, training with the Hughes AGM-65A TV-guided, fire-and-forget Maverick officially got underway on 22 June 1973 with the F-4E-equipped 334th TFS *Eagles* at Seymour-Johnson AFB, North Carolina. Within seven years it had become the principal air-to-surface missile of the Phantom fraternity, including the F-4G 'Wild Weasels', one of whose jets is here seen taxying at Spangdahlem in 1980 equipped with a TGM-65B 'Scene Mag' training round. (Lindsay T. Peacock)

▶ A TGM-65B training round (possessing a working seeker for practice lock-ons) is hauled along the flight-line at Nellis AFB, Nevada, during 'Red Flag 84-4'. The TV-guided Maverick is used by all three US Services (which expended some 5,300 rounds of all marks during Operation 'Desert Storm') and has been exported worldwide. The first overseas customers included Israel, South Korea and Switzerland. (Frank B. Mormillo)

▼ Cutaway of the Maverick missile, showing the principal differences between the 125lb- and 300lb-warhead versions and the chief forms of guidance. (Hughes Missiles)

GUIDANCE AND CONTROL SECTION — CENTER SECTION

AFT SECTION

ELECTRONICS

SAFE-ARM-FUZING THERMAL BATTERY

CONTACT SENSOR

DOME COVER

TV OR SCENE MAG TV SEEKER

LASER SEEKER

IR SEEKER

FORWARD FIRING SHAPED-CHARGE WARHEAD (125lb/57kg)

FUZE DELAY SELECT UNIT

BOOST-SUSTAIN SOLID PROPELLANT ROCKET MOTOR

FLIGHT CONTROL SURFACES

KINETIC ENERGY PENETRATOR BLAST-FRAGMENT WARHEAD (300 lb/136 kg)

SAFETY/ARMING DEVICE

MEASURES		WEIGHTS	
LENGTH	98 in./249 cm	A/B	462 lb/210 kg
DIAMETER	12 in./30.5 cm	D	485 lb/220 kg
WING SPAN	28.5 in./72 cm	E	645 lb/293 kg
		F/G	675 lb/307 kg

and those of the follow-on models described presently, built by a Hughes subsidiary in LaGrange, Georgia, have also been adopted as standard homing devices for a plethora of weapons.[2]

Satisfying the fighter commanders' needs for a round-the-clock, limited adverse-weather version was the next challenge—to meet the threat of advanced Soviet-designed armour which was creeping inexorably forward into night-time operations by means of cheap starlight and night vision devices, enabling their drivers to negotiate forests, open bogland and even rivers under the cloak of darkness before bivouacking under stealthy camouflage netting. Without such a capability, it was argued, mass formations of tanks, deadly ZSU-23/4 mobile AAA and tracked SAM-6 batteries would be able to grind relentlessly across NATO's Fulda Gap. Amongst the Army staff this realization revitalized memories of a weather-grounded air force which had been unable to act as a buttress against the Nazi heavy armour that ploughed its way through the Belgian Arden-nes during the Battle of the Bulge in the autumn of 1944. Moreover, a night-capable Maverick, peering through the darkness and smoke (though not yet rain, clouds or fog), which would capitalize on the emerging tech-nology of the expendable imaging infra-red seeker with its hot-on-cold and cold-on-hot sensing characteristics, would enable the fighter-bomber crews to pick out lucrative targets easily on their dual-mode DSRCs (digital-scan radarscope converters, adapted to flash-up radar or E-O imagery on *one* cathode ray tube), permitting fairly good dis-crimination between dummy and *bona fide* targets and between active, warm radar dishes and ones that may have been liter-ally knocked-out cold; and to place the crosshairs on choice POL storage facilities, the quantity of oil or gasoline remaining in a fuel hold, for example, being readily visible. Quizzed on this facet of infra-red technology, an Intruder NFO from VA-65 *Tigers* described the seekers as 'Marvel Comic "X-Ray specs"'.[3] After a shaky start, mostly as a result of understandably heavy scrutiny of its field trials performance in the high humidity and cold of the customary late autumn and early spring European exercises, the IIR version was ordered into production as the AGM-65D. Painted in a new drab green livery, initial lots joined the USAF inventory during 1983 and achieved IOC with the A-10As of the 81st TFW *Blue Dragons* three years later. It has also since been manufactured for the US Navy as the AGM-65F, and as a follow-on model for its originator as the -65G, both of which feature 300lb blast-fragmentation warheads.

The chief exponents of both the television and infra-red guided Mavericks are the USAF's 'tank-busting' OA/A-10A 'Warthogs', which accounted for 90 per cent of the 5,300, £70,000-apiece missiles expended in the Gulf. A gross of 'Hogs', drawn from seven squadrons from RAF Alconbury in England, Myrtle Beach in South Carolina and England AFB and NAS New Orleans in Louisiana, were forward-deployed to Damman/King Fahd in Saudi Arabia, from where the lizard-green 'European One' aircraft generated 8,500 sorties, the Mavericks assisting in the destruction of more than 1,000 tanks, 1,200 artillery pieces and 2,000 vehicles. The units also scouted for Scuds (lending them the nickname 'Scud Hogs'), attacked enemy air defences ('Wart Weasels') and hit a couple of enemy helicopters ('Wart Eagles'). Triple-rail LAU-88 and single-rail LAU-117 launchers were both used, in conjunction with a mix of TV- and infra-red-guided Mavericks. Production contracts have been issued to replenish the inventory, while sales overseas via Hughes and second-source supplier Raytheon continue at a lively pace.

THE MAVERICK FAMILY

Type	Guidance	Warhead	Chief user	Production
AGM-65A	TV (5° FOV)	125lb shaped	USAF	1972–75
AGM-65B	TV Scene-Mag	125lb shaped	USAF	1975–83
AGM-65C	Laser	125lb shaped	USAF	Development only
AGM-65D	Imaging IR	125lb shaped	USAF	1983–87
AGM-65E	Laser	300lb blast-frag	USMC	1985–present
AGM-65F	Imaging IR	300lb blast-frag	USN	1987–present
AGM-65G	Imaging IR	300lb blast-frag	USAF	1989–present

Notes: TV models use the clear DSU-27/B seeker, imaging infra-red versions the silvery WGU-10/B seeker. These are 'common' units which are also employed in the GBU-15(V) glide bomb and its rocket-powered derivative the AGM-130A, and the AGM-84 SLAM. TGM-65D/F/G training round seekers have a milky metallic yellow-orange appearance, and all TGM rounds lack the rear steering fins.

When Maverick is not man enough for the job, the USAF and its allies can draw on heftier PGMs which share the same guidance. The biggest in the arsenal are the American Rockwell AGM-130A and Israel's Rafael Popeye. The AGM-130A is a straightforward adaptation of the short-chord, one-ton GBU-15(V)-2/B, boosted by a strap-on rocket motor which gives it a range of 12–25 miles

◀ A USAFTAWC F-16C fires an AGM-65G Maverick during follow-on operational weapons trials over the Eglin Munitions Systems Division range in Florida. The AGM-65G has demonstrated a pK of 90 per cent. (Hughes Missiles)

(depending again on launch altitude). Its guidance works in precisely the same manner as that of the GBU-15 glide bomb series, with a fly-it-to-target option via a Hughes AN/AXQ-14 video data-link. Not cleared for use in time for combat during 'Desert Storm', the weapon is now entering service with the USAF's rapidly expanding cadres of F-15E Strike Eagles under the 4th Wing at Seymour-Johnson AFB, North Carolina, and the newly re-equipped *Statue of Liberty* Wing at RAF Lakenheath in England. The B-52G 'Buff' may also be fitted with the Popeye, built under licence in the United States by Martin Marietta as the AGM-142A 'Have Nap'. This will remain one of the aircraft's primary stores when the aged force of thirty-three remaining jets is reconsolidated at K. I. Sawyer AFB in Michigan under the new Air Combat Command during 1994–95. The weapon shares much in common with the other electro-optic guided bombs and missiles in terms of technology, but it combines that with a staggering sixty-mile range—reminiscent of the advanced British Martel AJ168 and several similar American

◄ The AGM-65D imaging infra-red-guided Maverick introduced a night-time and limited adverse-weather capability to the series, plus a new olive green colour scheme. Operational units began to receive the weapon in 1983. Production has now switched to the 'Golf' model, which replaces the original forward-firing, shaped-charge 125lb warhead with a new, more devastating 300lb blast-fragmentation version. (Hughes Missiles)

► The GBU-15(V)2/B and -15I models featuring the later MXU-787 aerofoil 'groups' have been transformed into the AGM-130 stand-off missile by means of a strap-on rocket motor, effectively increasing low-altitude range to twelve miles and high-altitude range to around thirty. In partnership with the Maverick and GBU-15 glide bomb series, the weapons use the USAF-common DSU-27/B TV and WGU-10/B imaging infra-red seekers. This particular example is bolted to an F-15E Strike Eagle, one of several engaged in 'Seek Eagle' weapons trials at Eglin AFB, Florida. (Rockwell International)

projects which were axed in the 1970s (the Rockwell AGM-53 TV-guided Condor and the same company's planar-wing 2,000lb GBU-20 glide bomb among them). 'Have Nap' was purchased originally as a stop-gap measure when the AGM-130A was encountering difficulties during test drops, but impressive stocks of both types now exist. Available for combat when hostilities broke out in the Gulf, the AGM-142A 'Have Nap' was kept securely on the ground throughout the Gulf War to mollify members of the Arab coalition forces, who expressed strong objections to its allies' employing weapons of Israeli origin! Adequate substitutes were provided by the US Navy SLAM, described below. Even newer systems currently gestating in the United States include the rocket-powered Northrop AGM-137 Tri-Service Stand-off Attack Missile (TSSAM), a stealthy missile spawned by Project 'Have Slick' which has been under secret development since 1986, and the Navy/Texas Instruments Advanced Interdiction Weapons System (AIWS). These are designed to be launched from up to 375 miles away, outside the effective range of the enemy's anti-aircraft defences, and can be built up in modular fashion with a variety of submunitions and guidance sections, in 'pick 'n' mix' fashion, to meet the needs of the 'Weaponeers'. The chief users will include the angular F-117A, the sea-going F/A-18C and A-6E and the venerable B-52H, though the RAF and several other prospective export clients have expressed genuine interest.

▲ The AGM-130 received a thorough work-out at Eglin before being cleared for series production, just too late to be used during 'Desert Storm'. Here a 3246th Test Wing F-111E tries out four of them. (Rockwell International)

LASER MISSILES

Other forms of guidance also exist for Maverick and its cousins. Gulf bombing by the Buccaneers highlighted some of the shortcomings of Paveway 'smart' bombs. The venerable ladies and their crews performed admirably, but during the strikes against the bridges spanning the Euphrates near Fallujah, several CPU-123/B LGBs missed their aimpoints. LGBs nearly always guide in the right azimuth, as the seeker-canard combination can self-compensate for wind, but on occasion they have a tendency to fall 'long' or 'short' of the target, especially if designation commences too early, causing the seeker to 'look down' too soon and reduce the weapon's ballistic range, or when the bomb is released at the edge of its delivery envelope. Aware of this shortcoming for several years, the US Navy contracted

◄ The US Navy has for a long time been the world's leader in the development of precision-guided missiles. The AGM-53 Condor programme of the mid-1970s was no exception: this impressive Rockwell device had an effective range of up to 60 miles! The centreline pod mounted on this A-6 is a data link system for stand-off communication with the Condor's TV seeker (identical in concept to the Walleye/SLAM AN/AWW-9 and GBU-15/AGM-130 AN/AXQ-14 pods). Four A-6Es were rigged to carry the weapon, as was one F-4J Phantom, but it was cancelled in favour of earth-hugging, conventionally armed BGM-109 cruise missiles. (Rockwell International)

Emerson Electric to strap a Shrike rocket motor on to the rear of the 1,000lb GBU-16/B, to create the 'Skipper II'. This provides an extra measure of stand-off range—up to 5 miles—while at the same time ensuring that the bomb has enough energy to reach its target. AGM-123A Skipper IIs joined the US Navy's A-6E squadrons during 1987 and were used successfully for the first time in April the following year by A-6Es of VA-95 *Green Lizards* during Operation 'Praying Mantis', an American 'protective reaction' strike against Iranian Navy gunboats which were perceived as posing a threat in the Straits of Hormuz. During the attack, one of the LGBs disappeared down the frigate *Sablan*'s funnel, at the time speeding merrily along at 30–35kt, and stopped it dead in the water! Further examples were expended during 'Desert Storm' by Intruders and Hornets flying from the Red Sea but never with quite the startling effects demonstrated during the weapon's combat début!

Another solution was adopted by the US Marines, which took the USAF's experimental AGM-65C laser Maverick and updated it into the 'Echo' model. This was the first member of the family to introduce the beefier 300lb blast-fragmentation warhead—still modest compared to the Skipper II, but with more than double the clout of the original Maverick. The warhead has since been adopted by the US Navy and US Air Force for their imaging infra-red models, creating the 'Foxtrot' and 'Golf' derivatives respectively. France has also followed this line of thinking with its Aérospatiale AS30L-for-Laser missile. This was developed from the basic *Air-Sol* 30 series which had its origins as the radio-controlled Nord model 5401 (similar in philosophy to the obsolete American Bullpup), and fully fledged tests began in late 1977 at Cazaux, the nation's chief weapons development centre located just south of the Basin d'Arcachon near Bordeaux. Laser illumination was provided by the Cilas ITAY-71

▼ Rafael of Israel developed the Condor concept into the Popeye, a sixty-mile-range TV-guided missile steered to target via data link pod. It is being manufactured under licence by Martin Marietta in the United States, for use on the USAF's ageing B-52G strike force. This 'Buff', from Combat Command's 2nd Bomb Wing, carries two of the weapons, designated the AGM-142 Have Nap. Because of its Israeli origins it was not employed during 'Desert Storm'—such insensitivity may have caused cracks in the delicate Coalition structure. (Martin Marietta)

◄ Brunswick developed the Low Altitude Dispenser (LAD) as a stand-off submunitions delivery technology demonstrator. It evolved into the rocket-powered Modular Stand-off Weapon (MSOW) but was cancelled in favour of the latest 'stealthy' Tri-Service Stand-off Attack Missile (TSSAM) and 'Have Slick' weapons, which will enter service in the mid-1990s. (Brunswick Defense)

'gun' contained in the now widely employed ATLIS 2 pod. This combination represented the world's first autonomous laser missile package to be employed by a single-seat aircraft. Operational deliveries began in 1983, with exports going to Iraq for use against Iran in the bloody *Jihad*. Ironically, Iraq also became the recipient of the sharp end of the AS30L during the Gulf War when *Armée de l'Air* Jaguar As flying from Al Ahsa fired sixty of the missiles against POL and ammunition dumps and other fixed targets dotted around

Kuwait! An 80 per cent accuracy was demonstrated, despite intense fire which must have proved a distraction to the pilots.

Fiercest, yet most petite, of all the laser-guided missiles is the US Army/Rockwell International AGM-114 Hellfire (Helicopter-launched, fire-and-forget) missile, up to sixteen of which can be carried at a time in four-packs under the wing stubs of the spirited AH-64A Apache gunship helicopter.[4] Hellfire was developed in concert with the hugely successful Apache beginning in 1972, and

full go-ahead was authorized four years later. The weapon uses a Martin Marietta Cassegrain telescope laser seeker which consistently enables the missile, in the words of former US Assistant Secretary for Defense Bill Perry, to go 'right through the centre of the bull's-eye'. Designation is provided by the helicopter's helmet-linked Martin Marietta Target Acquisition Designation Sight and Pilot's Night Vision Sensor (TADS/PNVS), which operate as the 'eyes' of the crew when flying by night or in hazy weather. On paper, Hellfire is effective at ranges of up to 5 miles—twice that of the latest wire-guided Hughes BGM-71E TOW 2A—though typical engagements are conducted at closer quarters.

The first production Hellfires were delivered in September 1984 and manufacture by Rockwell International and second-source supplier Martin Marietta has now exceeded 30,000 rounds. The missile packs a tiny but lethal 14lb shaped-charge warhead. This features a cone of copper that collapses inward on detonation to form a narrow jet of liquid metal, which, in demonstrations conducted at Eglin AFB, Florida,

penetrated four feet of earth and $2\frac{1}{2}$ft of reinforced concrete, shattered the interior of a bunker and then went on to poke through $5\frac{1}{2}$ft more concrete and earth—a nasty device by anyone's reckoning. The latest in the series, the AGM-114F, also overcomes the counterforce created by Soviet 'reactive armour' plating by using two charges, the first to negate the coating and the second to penetrate tank hulls (or to cause pieces of metal and miscellany in the tank's interior to break loose and fly around its cabin). The effects are better left to the imagination.

Hellfire can be let loose in LOBL and LOAL launch modes, the former where there is direct line-of-sight to target for the Apache's TADS/PNVS and the latter preparatory to a helicopter 'pop' or when designation is provided by infantry or companion scouts acting as 'buddies', permitting it to be fired from behind cover: post launch, it ascends to 1,000ft before its supersonic descent on to the 'spot' of the illuminated target. This enables it to bypass the tougher frontal and flank armour of its quarry, though it is equally adept at penetrating the chunky turrets of the best armour, according to the US Army. In

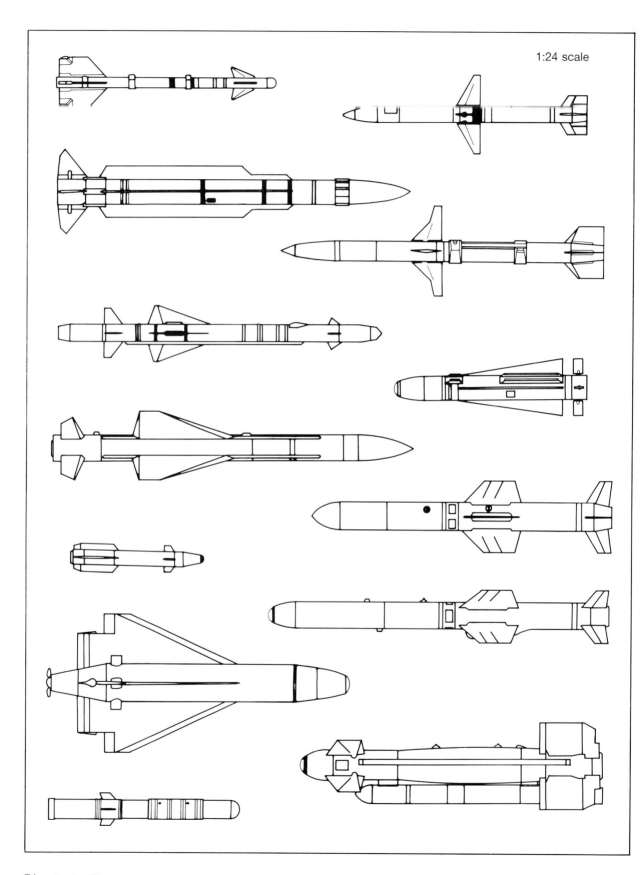

▲ An AH-1S squats on its skids with its engine compartment open to reveal the basics of the AH-1S Cobra's Avco Lycoming T53-L-703 turboshaft engine. The armament comprises an M261 rocket launcher and a pair of BGM-71F TOW 2B anti-tank missile launchers. Note also the Sanders AN/ALQ-144 'disco light' infra-red countermeasures emitter sprouting just aft of the rotor mount. (Author)

◄ Air-to-surface missiles. Left, top to bottom: AGM-122 Sidearm anti-radar missile; AGM-78D-2 Standard ARM; ALARM; AM39 Exocet anti-ship missile; AGM-114 Hellfire laser-guided anti-tank weapon; AGM-62 ERDL 'Fat Albert' Walleye TV-guided bomb; and BLU-107/B Durandal anti-runway weapon. Right, top to bottom: AGM-45A-10 Shrike ARM; AGM-88B/C HARM; AGM-65B-G Maverick; AGM-84 Harpoon anti-ship missile; AGM-84E SLAM; and AGM-130 rocket-assisted 'Short Chord' GBU-15(V)-2/B. (Author)

practice, Hellfires are launched in one of three primary modes—single shot, 'rapid fire' or 'ripple fire'. The rapid fire sequence discharges the missiles at 8-second intervals, during which time the coded TADS/PNVS laser designator can be shifted about to 'zap' different targets or to concentrate firepower on a 'tough nut'. Ripple fire, at 1–2-second intervals, permits a barrage of missiles to home in on the reflected laser energy of up to two designators, tracking two or more targets in a flurry of firepower. These features bring maximum weaponry to bear with the shortest possible exposure to enemy defences. In the Gulf, the Hellfire proved awesome. Apaches were the first aircraft to open fire in the conflict when they were dispatched deep into Iraqi lines preparatory to the main strike waves to knock out early warning radars. Diverting their attention shortly afterwards to Iraqi armour, the Apache brigades ended the war with confirmed claims on more than 500 tanks, 120 armoured personnel carriers, 120 artillery pieces, 30 AAA sites and twenty aircraft destroyed. Not surprisingly, post-Gulf sales of the deadly Apache-Hellfire combination

have rocketed, in both senses of the word! Work is currently well under way on a dual-mode millimetre wave (MMW) seeker operating in the high part of the RF spectrum, capable of autonomous operation based on preprogrammed target 'signatures'. This same guidance technology is also opening up as a 'fail safe' option for Maverick, the Paveway IV PGMs and numerous 'smart' submunitions contained in the latest CBU developments. They will likely bloom in the West's military inventories during the latter half of this decade.[5]

GETTING THE BOAT

Anti-shipping, or 'Getting the Boat' as the job is known to those crews assigned to the task, was for a long time one of the most hazardous duties undertaken by aviators. The mission was first combat proven during Operation 'Judgement', the Royal Navy's daring Swordfish torpedo attack against the Italian Fleet at Taranto in November 1940. The mission gained notoriety during the 'Day of Infamy' on 7 December 1941, when the Japanese struck the US Pacific Fleet at its home port, Pearl Harbor, and sucked the

◀ The Aérospatiale AM39 Exocet achieved notoriety during the 1982 Falkland Islands campaign, when Argentine Super Etendards toting one weapon, a 'buddy' refuelling pod and a drop tank (a configuration identical to the one demonstrated by this *Aéronavale* example) crippled *Sheffield* and *Atlantic Conveyor*. Exocet may also be helicopter-launched from larger machines like the Super Frelon. (Dassault Aviation)

◀ The McDonnell Douglas AGM-84 Harpoon, the 'American Exocet', has also claimed sea-going victims. It was first used in combat by A-6E Intruders of VA-34 *Blue Blasters* on the night of 24 March 1986, when the 260-ton Libyan fast patrol boat *La Combattante* was sunk. Overseas export customers include Australia, and here four Harpoons are seen bolted to one of her ARDU (Air Research Development Unit) F-111C 'swingers', which are tasked with both overland and sea strike duties. (RAAF)

United States into the global conflagration. Within two years the nature of this new form of warfare had escalated into mallet blows between aircraft carriers, well out of gun range of one another. The US Navy's defeat of its Japanese opponents in May and June 1942 at the Battles of the Coral Sea and Midway marked the turning point, and anti-shipping strikes reached a furious climax during operations against Okinawa, when ships battled against *kamikazes*. This style of naval warfare set a pattern of training which remained valid for a further thirty-five years, as the world's wealthier nations honed naval air power and gradually decommissioned their big battleships. Steel 'flat tops' of comparatively vast acreage became the new capital ships, festooned with expensive jets capable of hunting and destroying smaller surface craft and submarines alike, and of engaging one another in potentially fierce battles. The task remained ever hazardous for the flyers. Open sea provides no cover to mask one's approach, or from behind which to 'toss' a bomb. Attacking a ship meant first running the gauntlet of the enemy's sophisticated long-range radar-directed defences, then its murderous flak. As the cost of aircraft, and training crews to the standards required, rose ever higher, it became increasingly necessary to devise more intelligent ways of dealing with enemy shipping—other than by simply escalating what might be a small conflict into a nuclear confrontation with the first blow.[6]

The solution was the missile, demonstrated with harrowing success when, on 4 May 1982, the radar picket ship HMS *Sheffield* was hit amidships by a sea-skirting Aérospatiale AM39 Exocet launched from a Super Etendard belonging to *No. 2 Escuadrilla de Caza y Ataque* of the *Comando de Aviacion Naval Argentina* (CANA). The crippled destroyer sank six days later, and sent shudders through the world's navy chiefs, a feat which was repeated on 27 May when the *Atlantic Conveyor* was destroyed by one of another pair of Exocets, also launched from Super Etendards flying from Rio Grande on the mainland. The one redeeming factor for the British fleet was that CANA by this time had used four of its *total* inventory of five Exocets; the outcome of the war may have been far bloodier if more of the deadly missiles had been available—'the luck and draw of war', as Sea Harrier pilot 'Sharky' Ward

described events. The inevitable consequences of this first series of encounters was a budding market in anti-missile missiles, distracting radar reflectors and advanced chaff 'blooming' devices (some of them marketed by ex-Sea Harrier pilots, 'Sharky' among them, who had been on the receiving end!), but an equally fruitful one in anti-ship missiles, which are becoming increasingly cunning.

Exocet, the pioneer, was put into production in 1974 for air-launch from the *Aéronavale*'s Super Frelon helicopters on which they entered service in July 1977, followed a year later by marriage with the Super Etendard. Air launch obviates the need for a booster to get the weapon up to initial speed, but its employment still demands a certain cool: the fighter first 'pops' from a wave-hugging, radar-avoiding flight posture to acquire the enemy on radar, then hands the target over to the missile before descending, out of line-of-sight with the target's radar defences. Exocet is then let free at a range of over 30 miles from its intended victim, ignites its SNPE Helios smokeless rocket motor one second later and dashes towards the known target at Mach 0.93, as low as 8ft from the ocean waves—a precocious device, which frees its carrier to 'knock it off' and head for home. Once in the vicinity of the target, it switches on its active EMD Adac X-band radar to search for the quarry, locks on and then homes in to deliver a 364lb hexolite/steel block blast-fragmentation penetrating warhead.[7] The $1 million missile's 50 per cent success rate at defeating $250 million ships in the Falklands conflict prompted sales way in excess of its reliability, albeit restricted by an uncharacteristically guilt-stricken French government to a mere six select countries.

The US Navy's equivalent, first demonstrated against target ships nine years prior to the Falklands Campaign, is the McDonnell Douglas AGM-84 Harpoon, which until very recently was the only satisfactory supplement to the sledgehammer nuclear anti-ship, anti-submarine bombs and depth charges available to the Fleet's P-3 Orion and S-3 Viking sea-going aircraft.[8] Powered by an air-breathing Teledyne CAE J402 turbojet, which furnishes an impressive range of over fifty miles, Harpoon first saw action during Operation 'Prairie Fire' with the US Navy's Sixth Fleet in the Gulf of Sirte on

24–25 March 1986, when A-6E Intruders from VA-34 *Blue Blasters* and VA-85 *Black Falcons* sank three Libyan patrol craft. The 260-ton *La Combattante* and a pair of 780-ton 'Nanuchka 2' class patrol boats were struck from beyond a range of 30 miles, well outside the boats' 'Ganef' SAM defensive umbrellas. As one of the pilots involved remarked at the time, 'I doubt if the Libyans saw it coming'. It was his first-ever Harpoon launch.

Fitted with an active radar and a 488lb warhead, Harpoon works very much like Exocet and has similarly been progressively improved as production shifts up the alphabet of marks. The latest is the AGM-84D, which shares much in common with the latest AM39 (and similar Israeli Gabriel III, British BAe Dynamics Sea Eagle and German MBB Kormoran, none of which has been air-launched in combat). Despite its sophisticated programming, target discrimination has yet to be sharpened and, when presented with plenty of lucrative targets, the weapons behave 'like polecats in a duck coop'. The genuine fear that 'friendlies' might have been hit precluded their use in the Gulf—except for the very different 'spin-off' AGM-84E SLAM (Standoff, Land-Attack Missile). This is a stretched Harpoon fitted with the imaging infra-red seeker from the Maverick and the LOAL video data-link equipment from the ER/DL Walleye, designed to strike fixed land-based targets. VA-75 *Sunday Punchers* A-6Es from the USS *John F. Kennedy* introduced the weapon to combat with seven launches, guided from afar via AN/AWW-9 data-link pods carried by A-7Es from the sister squadrons. Four hit their targets smack-on, some in trail: Rear Admiral Conrad C. Lautenbacher coolly described such a sequence of events during the video replays at Riyadh, but a Navy 'SLUF' pilot responsible for the data-link TV control from the air hit the nail on the head: 'My eyes were like *this* big watching the second missile go into the first hole'!

IRON HAND

Most notorious of all targets are the opponent's anti-aircraft defences, particularly the sophisticated radar-directed ones which guide SAMs and Triple-A with disturbing precision—both from land and from shipborne batteries. Air crews who confront these do so with a mixture of heightened fear and satisfaction, aware both of the inherent dangers involved and of the protection they are affording their colleagues. During the turbulent war in South-East Asia, the job adopted the generic trade name 'Iron Hand'. US Navy crewmen, customarily assigned to the task on an *ad hoc* basis in support of their

▼ A *Cheyl Ha'Avir* F-4E tucks up its landing gear, outbound with a pair of Israeli Aircraft Industries Gabriel III anti-ship missiles. Like the Exocet and Harpoon, Gabriel uses an active radar seeker to acquire and lock on to its target, after having been set on course at a stand-off range of 30–40 miles by the launch aircraft. (Israeli Aircraft Industries)

▲ A pair of F-105G 'Weasel Thuds' from the 116th TFW *Georgia Rebels* roll in on the target with finless TGM-45 Shrike training rounds. The AGM-45A was developed in response to the radar threats encountered over Cuba in 1962 and is still operational today. (Lindsay T. Peacock)

◄ Britain's solution to the stand-off anti-shipping requirement is the BAe Dynamics Sea Eagle, which equips Royal Navy Sea Harriers and RAF Buccaneer S.2s. Like the competition, it is hefty weapon designed to be launched at a stand-off range of up to 'several tens of miles', but this type has not seen any combat. Norway, too, has developed a highly-capable anti-ship 'shooter', the AGM-119B Penguin. (BAe Dynamics)

Carrier Air Groups, referred to the task as 'flying shotgun'; USAF crews, specially selected and trained for the role as strike escorts and who worked under the motto 'First In, Last Out!', became known as the 'Wild Weasels'.[9] Both services introduced the concept using different aircraft and tactics, but both shared one common denominator—the array of weaponry at their disposal.

First into the inventory was the NOTS ASM-N-10 Shrike, named after that small bird which ruthlessly impales its insect victims on a thorn. Development, which began in 1958, was accelerated after the American encounters with Soviet-manned SAM sites in Cuba, which downed one U-2 and peppered several other recce machines. Production by Texas Instruments began in 1963, by which time the missile had been redesignated AGM-45, in good time for the 'Rolling Thunder' campaign against North Vietnam. This used a fixed seeker pre-tuned to the envisaged radar threat and was typically fired within 5 miles of the threat, despite the fact that maximum ballistic range was at least double that; the goal, as prescribed during early engagements, was to 'keep heads down'. This permitted friendly aircraft to go about their business striking primary targets

uninterrupted, while 'Weasel' or 'Iron Hand' wingmen sneaked in on the enemy radar sites, lobbed Shrikes and then followed up with cluster munitions and 'iron' bombs.[10]

Soon after the introduction of Shrike, the North Vietnamese began placing their 'Fan Song' and 'Fire Can' radars on 'dummy' standby status between bursts of activity. Quickly computed radar pot-shots were then fired just as the Americans were on their attack runs, too late for an ARM counter-attack. Counter-strategies were evolved, leading rise to the so-called 'cat and mouse game' (known more appropriately nowadays as the 'duelling mongoose and cobra'), which continued unabated throughout the aerial offensives. One was for the 'Iron Hand' machines to break formation from the strike package at some distance from the coast-in or initial points and 'nav loft' launch up to four AGM-45s towards the suspected sites, 2–3 seconds apart, while climbing parabolically up to 45° pitch. The missiles then careered skywards in a vertical fan to descend and diverge in the vicinity of suspected outlying sites, just as the 'friendlies' began their attack runs at fixed times and headings. Other, more sophisticated techniques were employed by the nineteen A-6B Intruders specially adapted to the 'Iron Hand' role.[11]

◄ The small Shrike is ideally suited to today's diminutive fighters such as the F-16. This olive green TGM-45A-9 training round, depicted here without its fins fitted, is used for captive practice 'lock ups' on 'enemy' radar sites. (Author)

These aircraft bristled with superheterodynes and interferometers which 'sniffed' the air-waves, often in conjunction with an activated ARM seeker, to plot the radar positions. For example, the A-6B's P-8 computer pro-gramme, introduced in 1969, permitted the aircraft to range-find with the fixed Shrike seeker: after having taken a bearing to the target, the Intruder would enter into a gentle turn 20–30° left or right, then line up again on the enemy. The two bearings were used by the Bomb-Nav-Computer to triangulate the position of the target, which could then be engaged using automatic missile launch at the optimum range and subsequently flashed-up on the DVRI (Direct View Radar-scope Indicator) tube to permit the navigator to set up the switches for a 'radar bombs' delivery. This technique, known as PAT-ARM (Passive Angle Tracking via ARM), was one of many employed. For the most part, however, Shrike was a see-him-and-shoot-him device which required 'mixing it up' at close quarters, often after first having *overflown* the site! Production closed during 1981 with 600 of the AGM-45A-10, bringing the total produ-ced to 18,500 rounds in ten varieties equip-ped with thirteen different pre-tuned seekers. It remains in use to this day, but primarily as a 'cheap and cheerful' means of getting the enemy to shut down his radars temporarily.[12]

A better solution came in the form of the General Dynamics Pomona Standard ARM (known to US Navy crews as the STARM), which possessed a genuine stand-off range of up to 35 miles. Developed from 1966 based on the US Navy's Standard surface-to-air missile which was refitted with the

Shrike's seeker to create the basic AGM-78A Mod. 0 model, STARM went into battle in March 1968 slung under the wings of the A-6Bs of VA-75 *Sunday Punchers* flying from the deck of the USS *Kittyhawk*. After a tenta-tive start, precipitated by advance propa-ganda which effectively decreed firing the

▼ An F-4E from the 480th TFS *Warhawks* shows off its live 'Weasel' armoury comprising three AIM-7E-2 Sparrow III AAMs and pair of AGM-45A Shrikes. Most US fighters are qualified to carry Shrike. (USAFE)

missile only when a 'kill' was guaranteed (in order to avoid embarrassment lest it fail), the US Navy introduced the more potent AGM-78B Mod. 1. This brought PAT-ARM techniques to the fore, made possible by a new gimballed broad-band Maxson seeker which could turn behind its chunky radome, thus permitting the attacker to set itself up for launch without flying straight into the threat or to take passive radar bearings without the need to change aircraft heading. It was the brainchild of Johns Hopkins University. Other clever features introduced on the new STARM included coloured smoke to mark the SAM complex, which typically was re-attacked at close quarters with CBUs and 'iron' bombs once its radar had been rendered impotent. The ultimate interface between aircraft and STARM was offered by half a dozen A-6Bs equipped with the superb AN/APS-118 TIAS (Target Identification and Acquisition System), introduced to the war zone by the US Navy during 1970. Its lethality was ably demonstrated by the US Marines: during their brief spring stint on the USS Coral Sea, VMA(AW)-224 Bengals fired 47 AGM-78Bs and destroyed a confirmed eighteen 'Fan Song' radar vans, without loss! The US Marine 'Mud Movers', often maligned by their full-time carrier-based peers, managed to synergize the necessary 'gung-ho' with the ability to adapt to new technology, so vital to this most dangerous of all trades.

In the post-Vietnam years STARM continued in production, seeing service in yet better configurations as the AGM-78C and -78D/D-2, which was married to the A-6E's

AN/AWG-21 special receiver and the sophisticated IBM AN/APR-38 of the F-4G 'Advanced Wild Weasel'. However, these models were considered to be mere stop-gap measures pending the introduction of a successor. STARM was withdrawn wholesale from the US inventory by 1987, with a proportion of the stock going to Israel which possessed the survivors of twenty-two production Block 60–62 F-4E Phantoms adept at using it. STARM's key contribution, in capable hands, was to prove the sound-ness of the mission and act as the catalyst for the successful development of today's extra-ordinarily effective radar-killing missiles.

HARMERS AND ALARMISTS

STARM's greatest limitations were its large size and the need to interface it with complex avionics in order to maximize its potential, thus limiting its use to the select specialized heavyweights, the Thunderchief, Phantom and Intruder. There also existed a require-ment for an ARM which could outperform the opposing SAMs in a head-to-head encounter—hitting the enemy radar first so that its missiles will go 'ballistic'. Out of this 'wish list' the NWC defined the specifications

for its HARM (High-speed ARM). Develop-ment began in 1969 and, once at an advanced stage, was handed over in the customary Naval Systems Command fashion to a competent contractor. TI assumed responsibility for HARM in 1974 and pursued a well-structured full-scale development pro-gramme which took advantage of every new turn in technology.

Production deliveries commenced during 1981 and have been maintained at a steady pace ever since, with stocks peaking at around 10,000 weapons just prior to the out-break of hostilities in the Persian Gulf. The AGM-88A became fully operational with the sea-going forces of the Sixth Fleet during 1983 and first saw action on 24 March 1986 during 'Reaction Strikes' against Libyan SA-5 'Gammon' batteries at Sirte, which had been challenging US Navy aircraft who had dared (somewhat provocatively, it might be added) to cross Col. Qadaffi's notorious 'Line of Death' to tease his MiGs. Squads of F/A-18A Hornets from VFA-131 *Wildcats*, VFA-132 *Privateers*, VMFA-314 *Black Knights* and VMFA-323 *Death Rattlers*, all from the USS *Coral Sea*, scored direct hits with two HARMs and went on to suppress air

◄ A pair of semi-gloss F-4G 'Weasels' on the wing, each with its full complement of ARMs: the flagship from Lt. Col. George 'John Boy' Walton's 561st *Black Knights* in the slot position totes four AGM-45A-10 Shrikes; and the 37th TFW Wing aircraft, belonging to Col. Merril 'Ron' Karp, has four of the bigger and more lethal AGM-88A/B HARM. (USAF)

▼ During the first three days of 'Desert Storm' the F-4G 'Weasels' of the 35th TFW(P) at Sheik Isa, Bahrain, carried their full complement of 'wall-to-wall' HARMs. These two aircraft are being refuelled at one of the two dozen 'hot pits' at the base which were constantly replenished by a string of trucks trundling back and forth from Port Manoma. (USAF via Lt. Col. Jim Uken)

defences at Benghazi the following month with a further thirty missiles, during 'Iron Hand' operations in the ensuing Operation 'El Dorado Canyon'. In this original format the weapon was interfaced with the basic DECM (Defensive Electronic Countermeasures) of the US Navy's inventory of combat jets, working in two primary modes—'TOO' (target of opportunity), using its AWG-25 passive seeker to 'lock up' on threats unassisted, and 'Self Protect', whereby the system is interfaced with the DECM. Overall, the missile's firing parameters extend from tree-top and up, out to a range of 40 miles, with the capability of being programmed to turn through up to 180° after launch.

HARM is decidedly at its best when interfaced with the aged but capable Unisys AN/APR-47 modified F-4Gs of the USAF's élite 'Wild Weasels'—and the *Luftwaffe*'s 35-strong Tornado ECR (Electronic Combat-Reconnaissance) establishment which is now forming under *Jagdbombergeschwader* (JBG) *32* at Lechfeld and *JBG 38* at Jever. The new Tornados carry a similar kit to that of the 'Weasels', comprising a TI/Deutschland ELS (Emitter Location System). Using super-

sensitive 'sniffers', these aircraft are capable of plotting threat type, bearing and range for the optimum delivery of HARM both at close-quarters and at distance, with considerable target discrimination (a problem when lobbing the missiles from 'vanilla' fighters). This is made possible by the 'Pre Brief' mode, whereby the specifics (such as approximate location and frequency) of primary, secondary and even tertiary targets can be fed into the missile prior to take-off, based on elint data garnered prior to the mission.[13] This permits the HARM to be launched within its preferred 'launch footprint', approximately 25 miles from its intended prey, ready-tuned to 'zap' the opposition. If the primary goes off the air, the missile looks for its secondary threat, and so on; failing all three, it will revert to the 'TOO' mode and broaden its goals.

Beginning in April 1987, deliveries of the AGM-88B were made from TI's automated production facility. This obviated the need for the weapons to be returned to avionics depots for major reprogramming to counter unexpected new threats; instead, this task is accomplished on the flight-line or flight deck. The proof of the pudding came during Operation 'Desert Storm', where two thousand of the weapons were expended, some 66 per cent of them by the prestigious 'Wild Weasels' operating as part of the 4770th Combat Wing at Incirlik, Turkey, and the 35th TFW(P) at Sheik Isa, Bahrain. At the sharp end were the Bahrain-based 'Desert Weasel V Special Force' commanded by Col. Merril R. 'Ron' Karp, which comprised elements from Lt. Col. George 'John Boy' Walton's 561st TFS *Black Knights* from George AFB, California, and Lt. Col. Randy 'Wicks' Gelwix's 81st TFS *Panthers* from Spangdahlem, Germany. The units dispatched three dozen aircraft between 18 August and 5 September 1990, bolstered by extras from both bases during the height of the December festivities, during the final build-up of forces. These formed the backbone of the second and third waves of attacks on Iraq and Kuwait on day one of the air war, when US forces fired over 200 AGM-88A/Bs![14] Northrop BQM-74 Chukar drones had been sent in to 'flush out' the sites initially to confirm prewar elint. By day two the Iraqis were already respecting the 'Weasels' and were growing increasingly jittery in their scanning patterns for fear of being blasted by the HARMs, launched with the warcry 'Magnum!' This permitted Coalition aircraft to go about their business relatively unmolested. After day three the force switched from 'wall-to-wall' HARMs to a load of two missiles. Attri-

tion of further enemy electronic sites continued: the panoramic and homing indicators used by the 'Bears' in the pit of the F-4G, normally filled with 'trade', became increasingly blank as the enemy's electronic defences were slowly but inexorably consigned to oblivion, permitting the HARM-shooters to switch to three-hour-long 'Weasel Police' patrol tactics. Eventually, it became unnecessary even to launch missiles: when the 'Weasels' announced their presence using their beer brand callsigns, every enemy site within a respectable range

◀ Big HARM, little bird: an 'Electric Jet' from the *Fightin' Fifty-Second* clutches a HARM under each wing, strapped to an Aero-5A launch rail. Block 50 F-16Cs and specially adapted F-15E-cum-Gs will assume the 'Wild Weasel' mission beginning in 1994. F-16C 'Weasels' from the 23rd TFS *Fighting Hawks* flew limited operations during 'Desert Storm' out of Incirlik in Turkey. (Author)

◀ Capt. Pat Pence from the 81st TFS sends his love to Saddam! The Bahrain-based 'Weasels' fired over 1,100 HARMs against Iraqi radars. George's high-scorer was F-4G 69–7263, nicknamed 'No. 1 SAM-slammer', since adopted by Col. Merril 'Ron' Karp as his Wing ship. Spangdahlem's highest confirmed SAM-buster was 69–0250, with a dozen sites to its credit. (Lt. Col. Jim Uken)

▶ Northrop BQM-74C Chukar drones were launched on a one-way heading for Iraq during the opening manoeuvres of 'Desert Storm', their job being to act as bait to lure the enemy air defence systems on to the airwaves. (Northrop)

▼ BAe Dynamics have developed the ALARM for the RAF's Tornados, capable of zooming skyward to a height of over twelve miles before beginning to para-descend in a loiter mode. As soon as an appropriate enemy radar is activated, ALARM fires its second-stage rocket motor and plunges into the dish. This load of seven ALARMs is atypical, as is the yellow missile trials decor. (BAe Dynamics)

closed down! Owing to these terror tactics, no one yet knows precisely what the HARM's pK is: 'The results are being tabulated still, based on our claims and the other data'. Some aircraft (such as 69-7263, nicknamed 'No. 1 SAM-Slammer') and crews accounted for up to 37 HARMs fired each, 'assisting the more determined Iraqi radar operators with their wish to enter the Muslim equivalent of Valhalla'. Spangdahlem's top-scoring crew was EWO Maj. Ken Spaar and his pilot Capt. Vinnie Quinn, with a dozen confirmed 'kills'. Pilot Lt. Col. Ed Ballanco came in a close

second, with eleven sites notched up in concert with four different EWOs in his 'bear pit'.

Supplemental orders for 2,081 AGM-88Bs to replenish those expended during the war have already been placed, while plans are being mooted for the conversion of old stocks up to the latest 'Bravo' format. In the meantime, TI are pitching their third-generation AGM-88C-1 model against Loral Aeronutronic's similar C-2. Both sub-marks are designed to cope with modern frequency-hopping and the broader operating frequencies and modes deployed in today's 'electronic thickets'. Deliveries of the new version will commence in 1993, embracing a new warhead packing 10,000 tungsten-alloy cubes for added lethality. Exports so far include 600 to Germany for its ECR Tornado squads and unspecified quantities to Australia, Italy and Spain. Further orders are imminent.

Switching between radars so as to gain maximum intelligence with the minimum of exposure is a well known radar operator's trick, and one which will become ever more of a threat as state-of-the-art air defences make greater use of bistatic monopulse arrays (two or more geographically displaced radars which do not rely on easily jammed helical search, conical scan-and-track patterns). Perhaps better able to deal with this new cat-and-mouse game are the RAF and Saudi Tornados. BAe Dynamics developed the ALARM (Air-Launched Anti-Radiation Missile) precisely for this purpose, and it was fielded just in time to see action. Its key

advantage is that it offers significant 'radar harrassment' characteristics, made possible by its more varied launch modes: pre-brief (based on a tape load, and described as 'fly so many miles in that direction and look for such-and-such a radar'), and a loiter tactic whereby the missile soars up to 70,000ft before para-descending at a comparatively leisurely pace. The moment a potential target starts radiating, the missile dumps its chute, fires a rocket motor and charges into the radar.

Early problems with the Royal Ordnance Nuthatch motor were alleviated when Bayern Chemie of Germany stepped in with a replacement which fitted the bill. Loiter capability was first demonstrated in June 1990, when a test round was fired from an earth-hugging No. 32 Joint Trials Unit Tornado working out with the missiles at China Lake. By November, operational rounds, nine Tornados and properly briefed crews were winging their way to Tabuk in Saudi Arabia as part of the Operation 'Granby' build-up. Led

by Sqn. Ldr. Bob McAlpine of the specially formed No. 20 Sqn. ('*Alarmists*'), the unit eventually expended 121 rounds; the number would have been higher but for the fact that the unit ran out of missiles! Lead 'killer' was the appropriately named 'Alarm Belle' (ZD746), which flew a dozen successful ALARM missions, unleashing 31 missiles.

Suitably impressed by ALARM, the Saudi Arabians are buying an undisclosed number of the missiles as part of the multi-billion pound *Al Yamamah* deal. The inevitable 'bigger and better' American answer to ALARM, the Northrop AGM-136 'Tacit Rainbow' (based on a cruise missile design, which would offer $1\frac{1}{2}$ hours of loiter time), was recently axed owing to a number of intractable development problems. ALARM and HARM continue to rule the roost, their two quite different modes of employment proving to be complementary. The liaison between the '*Alarmists*' and the Weasels in Europe is very much alive and well, a year after hostilities ceased in the Gulf.

▲ Sporting three pale grey production ALARMs (the typical operational configuration prescribed by No. 20 Squadron), an RAF GR.1 awaits its next sortie at Tabuk, Saudi Arabia. Ten dozen of the missiles were launched by nine *Alarmist* Tornados. (Royal Air Force)

NOTES TO CHAPTER THREE

1. Refer to 'Iron Hand' and 'HARM and Alarmists', below, for a more detailed discussion of anti-radar missiles. RAF Buccaneers employed both types of Martel; *L'Armée de l'Air* used the AS37 version only.

2. The seekers also equip the various models of the GBU-15(V), AGM-84E SLAM and AGM-130A. Refer to Chapter 2 and see also below.

3. A-6Es possess some of the best infra-red imaging capabilities via their AGM-65F Mavericks

(described below) and TRAM sensor (described in Chapter 5), notwithstanding the fact that the AVTRs they used in the Gulf were not up to scratch compared to the recordings broadcast, post-mission, from their USAF, RAF and *Armée de l'Air* counterparts. This factor seriously misrepresented US Navy capability to the media and public alike. Refer to the Glossary and to Chapter 5 for a fuller account of infra-red technology. Primarily, aircraft sensors use FLIR to provide 'a full account of what's ahead' and the sensor compensates for varying heat-radiation intensities in order to render the overall image useful to the human eye; whereas imaging infra-red imagery used in weapons seekers is concerned more with identifying and holding lock on a specific contrast point, by means of a centroid compensator, whatever the surrounding activity. This is the fundamental if subtle difference between FLIR and IIR, which are easily confused.

4. Typical deadly stores combinations include eight Hellfires inboard and two outboard M261 2.75in rocket packs, the latter housing a total of 38 Mk. 66 projectiles capped with impact or penetrating fuses, or a like number of the new Mk. 70 Hydra.

5. A Hercules-designed MMW seeker was test-shot on a Maverick on 6 September 1991 at the Eglin range, guiding it to 'within a lethal distance' of a simulated air defence radar. This will soon be incorporated as a secondary guidance system. Such 'dual mode' technology increases the chances of a successful strike, but MMW is advancing at such a pace that it will soon be effective in its own right.

6. Refer to Chapter 4. US Navy sea-going patrol and carrier-borne aircraft enjoyed access to nuclear bombs and depth charges. They were removed at port following President Bush's famous announcement on 27 September 1991 of the US's nuclear alert step-down.

7. Fortunately for those of *Sheffield*'s sailors not stationed in the galley quarters, where the missile hit, this failed to explode. Instead, the ship was set alight by the Exocet's rocket motor, which spread its torment via the thick layers of paint in the ship's interior. Crews attempted to extinguish the flames but were eventually forced to abandon ship, on the Captain's orders. Considerable attention has since been directed at fire-resistant paint and fittings, and towards superior life-support, to be worn at all times during 'battle stations'.

8. Refer to Chapter 4.

9. 'Shotgun' was the callsign broadcast when a Shrike was launched, lest 'friendlies' mistook the ARM for an enemy SAM. The callsign for a Maverick launch is 'Rifle', and that for the new HARM (see below) is 'Magnum'.

10. Although few aircraft were actually felled by missiles (especially when compared to losses to optically aimed flak at the roll-in and pull-up points), the radars had an unnerving effect on strike performance. Moreover, crews would often be obliged to dump their bombs prior to rolling in on the target in order to outmanoeuvre the SAMs. A-6A/B crews referred to the North Vietnamese 'Playing the L-Band' in this psychological war. Weapons like Shrike, which

were intended to grate on the enemy's nerves as much as to destroy his radars, enabled air crews to go about their business with greater confidence—the crux of 'flying shotgun' or 'Weaselling'.

11. Including ten Mod. 0/1, three PAT-ARM and six TIAS models (described below). These A-6Bs were in such high demand that they were swapped at sea while their carriers entered Subic Bay in the Philippine for resupply and some R&R, between Line Periods of action in the South China Sea.

12. Shrike has also been used in combat by the Israelis. Their most successful SEAD mission was performed in the Syrian Beka'a on 9 June 1982, when nineteen radars were knocked out that afternoon using a combination of decoys, Shrikes, GBU-15s and STARMs (described below). The RAF, too, got a taste of Shrike during the preceding two weeks, when several were launched from special ADU-315 dual-Shrike adaptors fitted to a pair of Vulcan B.2s, which flew non-stop from Ascension Island to the Falklands, one at a time at three-day intervals. Operation 'Black Buck 4', the first in the series and launched on 28 May, was aborted five hours into the mission owing to a hose problem with its aerial refuelling tanker; 'Black Buck 5' got to the Islands on 31 May but claimed no 'kills'; then finally, on 3 June, 'Black Buck 6' successfully struck an Argentine Skyguard radar, though it was forced to divert to Rio de Janiero after its refuelling probe broke.

13. Based on elint data tape recorded during previous 'Weasel' scouting missions and on other data gleaned by TR-1As, EF-111As, RC-135s, ground posts and US Army and Navy aircraft. The United States operates the JEWC (Joint Electronic Warfare Center) at San Antonio, Texas, which is responsible for collating this information and preparing 'jamming strategies' and maps depicting a prospective enemy's Electronic Order of Battle, for use in various contingency operations.

14. Forming fifty 'Weasels' in Bahrain. Because of the age of the F-4Gs and their enormous operating costs, estimated to be three times that of a similar number of F-16C/Ds, the USAF recently made the bold decision to cut back its 'Wild Weasel' establishment to sixty F-4Gs and reassign a third of these to the Air National Guard at Boise, Idaho. The balance will serve as 'spare parts lockers' for the remainder of the fleet until they too are retired, between 1995 and 1997. A selected number of F-15Es are to be refitted with specialized HTS (HARM targeting system) electronics over the next two years and may carry the now traditional Weasel 'Golf' suffix, to create the F-15G. F-16Cs will act as 'companion Weasels', as they do today.

4.
WEAPONS OF ARMAGEDDON

ON 27 SEPTEMBER 1991 President George Bush announced that the aerial and ballistic missile forces of Strategic Air Command would cease all constant alert duties, bringing to an end the tense (and often boring) air and ground assignment that stretched back to 1 October 1957, when SAC CinC Gen. Power inaugurated the 'One-Third Ground Alert' system. As had been true in Britain for nigh on twenty-five years, only the strategic submarine forces would remain on constant vigil, 24 hours a day, 365 days a year. This directive extended to the few nuclear strikers left with the 'Victor Alert' assignment overseas, among them the F-16-equipped 512th FS *Pro Pace Vigilante* at Ramstein in Europe and the famous 8th FW *Wolfpack* at Kunsan in the Pacific Rim. As Chief of Staff Gen. Colin Powell put it at the subsequent Press briefing, 'We can now do conventionally much more efficiently things we thought we could do only with tactical nuclear weapons'. 'Desert Storm' was a vindication of this shift in policy, away from the NATO philosophy of 'Flexible Response' against possible Soviet aggression. Forces will retain a nuclear armoury reduced by nearly 50 per cent and will give up their strict regimes in favour of a muster which decrees dispatch at a comparatively leisurely 24 hours' notice—a delay which would have boiled the insides of some of the old SAC 'hard hats'! The continuing moral debates and political arguments that linger will swing to and fro for many years to come. What is, perhaps, more significant, is the shifting of attention more towards America's conception of an 'International Police Force', pack-

◄ Munitions technicians from the now defunct 380th Bomb Wing (Medium) configure an FB-111A's weapons bay with its nuclear cargo. The heavy duty MHU-83C/E loader is used for this purpose. (USAF)

ing plenty of firepower but state-of-the-art conventional weaponry, as opposed to the indiscriminate clout from the harnessed energy of the hydrogen bomb. Under this scenario, those few new nuclear devices in the pipeline are retreating more and more into the secret 'black world' back rooms, as 'Stealth', coupled with flexible pinpoint targeting, replaces obsolescent 'overkill'.

ENOLA GAY

Nuclear pioneers were the 509th *Enola Gay* Composite Group, which under the command of Col. Paul Tibbets and flying a select group of B-29 Superfortresses dropped the 'Little Boy' and 'Fat Man' *fission* bombs on Japan, to bring an abrupt and much-welcomed climactic conclusion to the Second World War. Prior to the strikes, the perception of those privy to the technology was that the 'A-Bomb' was simply a bigger bomb, and some even doubted that it would work. Adm. Bill Leahy, Chief of Staff to Roosevelt in March 1945, confided to the President that 'the atomic bomb will never go off, and I speak as an expert on explosives'! His aides reckoned it was wishful thinking; if air power was capable of delivering such blows, what would become of the Navy? Certainly, the aviators involved in those first two strikes had no idea of the power at their disposal. As 'Little Boy' left the bomb bay of 'Enola Gay' at 0815 on 6 August 1945, free-falling towards Hiroshima while its mother-ship promptly executed a 155° turn from the 'bombs away' co-ordinates to escape the glare and blast the crews had been briefed to expect, the astonished co-pilot, Capt. Bob Lewis, reported: 'There will be a short intermission while we bomb our target . . . *My God!*' From the rear gun position, TSgt. Bob Caron witnessed the simultaneous deaths of 78,000 Japanese people and the demolition of 48,000 buildings. The sometimes blasé attitude prevalent in the ever ebullient United States even prompted a farmer in Newport, Arizona, to write on 21 August 1945 to a non-existent 'Atomic Bomb Corp., Washington DC', and request: 'I have some stumps in my field that I should like to blow out. Have you any atomic bombs the right size for the job?'! Reflective Americans offered more sober commentaries following the first (and, thankfully, so far last) use of nuclear weapons in anger, while President Truman was brusque: 'If they [Japan] do not now accept our terms,

they may expect a rain of ruin from the air, the like of which has never been seen on this Earth'. Deterrence, as the concept would come to be known by, rests on a willingness to employ nuclear weapons; that the technology works is merely an adjunct to this. It was long ago when 'Enola Gay' (B-29 44-86292, today in storage under the custody of the Smithsonian) smashed Hiroshima and fellow-Superfort 'Bock's Car' (on display at the USAF Museum at Wright-Patterson, Ohio) pulverized Nagasaki, but we dare not forget the destructive power of the harnessed atom: the weapons described in other chapters of this book, employed as they have been with deadly consequences to those on the receiving end, are by comparison mere squibs.

THERMONUCLEAR BOMBS

In the aftermath of the Superfortress strikes came Operation 'Crossroads'. America wished to retain her new-found place in the world as a 'superpower' and met the task with typical enthusiasm, creating an *ad hoc* strategic nuclear force out of the institutional expertise developed at Los Alamos and under the auspices of the veteran 509th Bomb Group. In the space of just over fifteen years the newly created Strategic Air Command grew from a fledgeling force of B-29s to one boasting seventeen hundred giant shiny metal bombers, crewed and supported by a quarter of a million personnel. Alongside the huge new force, more powerful thermonuclear weapons (or hydrogen bombs, based on the *fusion* of light hydrogen isotopes of uranium and plutonium switched into the 'Runaway Super' mode by means of an atom-bomb 'trigger') 'upped the ante'. The theoretical groundwork began in 1942 concurrent with the establishment of the Los Alamos Laboratory and the 'Manhattan' Project, based on twenty years of study by physicists into the nuclear fusion processes involved in cosmic alchemy and stellar energy. By 1947 the 'Runaway Super' had advanced into Project 'Alarm Clock', and it soared after August 1949 when the Soviet Union joined the 'Atomic League' by setting off its first atomic bomb. This competition between the superpowers spurred a US Presidential Directive issued on 31 January 1950 which resulted in the necessary funding and resources to ensure the successful detonation of the world's first thermonuclear weapon—'Greenhouse George'—on 8 May 1951. From this emerged the gargantuan 21-ton Mk. 17, squeezed into the belly of SAC's giant B-36 Peacemakers (the only machines capable of delivering the device at that time), on which it achieved IOC in 1954. A succession of bombs and bombers ensued, employing modular weapons based on the commonly used Mk./B28 and Mk./B43, ranging from General Dynamics' supersonic B-58A Hustler (which would 'roll back' the defences with commensurately sleek B43 Mod. 1 thermonuclear bombs, four of which could be slung under the noisy giant's silver delta planform, before finishing off its intended primary target with a 'superpod' payload comprising a kerosene tank bolted to a 1-megaton H-bomb), to Britain's sleek, glossy white 'V-Bombers'—the Valiant, Victor and Vulcan—which stood on alert with equally impressive weapons, codenamed 'Blue Steel'.[1] These early devices offered yields of well over one megaton (or in excess of one million tons TNT equivalent explosive energy, *fifty times* the power of the 20-kiloton weapon dropped on Hiroshima), and to a certain extent were 'uncontrolled', a proverbial Pandora's Box: some of the physicists involved voiced reservations about whether or not the detonations might result in severe destruction to the planet. In fact, despite their massive explosive power, the bombs were far too inefficient at converting matter into energy to achieve this horrific result. The byproduct was a raging political discussion which has, over the years, become distorted by abandoned efforts into such mind-boggling projects as the neutron bomb—a device which kills people but leaves buildings intact. The truth remains that in this context 'a nuclear bomb is a bomb', and only its

yield, and the safety factors involved in 'okaying' it, and its use, have altered.

Tactical nuclear bombs (as opposed to strategic ones—although the distinction here, too, remains fuzzy) evolved further under the scrutiny of the American Atomic Energy Commission (now under the authority of the Department of Energy), whose developmental efforts were conducted in strict privacy in the subterra of the Nevada Desert at Tonopah in concert with Sandia National Laboratories (mirrored by British tests which crystallized sand in Australia). Everything that could carry a 'nuke' was designed to do so, not just the bombers, including several aircraft ill-suited to their 'cover' role of 'fighter' or 'attack' machine. Among these classic types were the single-seat models of the Douglas A-1 'Spad' and McDonnell Voodoo and the twin-seat North American Vigilante, the last two of which enjoyed more illustrious careers once remodelled into reconnaissance types. Delivery techniques similarly evolved from the high-altitude, level-drop, yank-the-stick-and-get-the-hell-out mode to more sophisticated ones at which the new fast-movers were proving adept. The departure into these more dynamic deliveries was 'lofting'—known to the aviators as the 'half-Cuban eight' or 'idiot loop' manoeuvre—which entailed a 6.5g pull-up at up to 70–75°, with automatic weapon release occurring at the apex, after which time the pilot executed an 'Immelman' wings-level recovery, to permit a dash out of the target area on a reciprocal heading. Meanwhile, the bomb would continue in a ballistic arc to an altitude of 25,000ft or so before descending on to the target. Lower-altitude delivery modes followed in the late 1950s, including the LABS (Low Altitude Bombing System)

▶ One of Boeing's famous 'Buffs' glistens in the sun, revealing its underwing armoury of four Douglas XGAM-87A Skybolt nuclear missiles, designed for use on the definitive 'Hotel' mark, and by Britain's Vulcan B.2 forces. Development began in 1958 and within three years trials rounds were making problem-free, extended-range flights. However, the missile was cancelled by US Secretary of Defense Robert McNamara in 1961, along with the B-70 Valkyrie bomber programme. (Boeing)

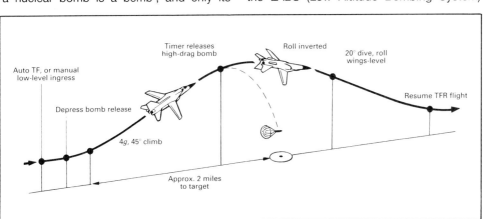

◀ Analogue F-111E LADD (Low Angle Drogue Delivery) profile used with the parachute-retarded B61 'silver bullet'. Digital aircraft practice a similar profile with Dual Bomb Timers (DBT). 'Idiot looping' or 'lofting' which was also employed, involved a steep climb with the bomb lobbed at the apex and the aircraft flipping on to its back, rolling wings level and departing on a reciprocal heading.

Timer releases high-drag bomb

Roll inverted

20° dive, roll wings-level

Auto TF, or manual low-level ingress

Resume TFR flight

Depress bomb release

4g, 45° climb

Approx. 2 miles to target

'toss', based on analogue timers for weapons release (cued into action at the Timer Reference Point, or Initial Point on the nuclear mission flight plan); and the faster, lower-angle LADD (Low Angle Drogue Delivery) and 'Lay Down' techniques introduced in the 1960s. These progressively *increased* the airspeed and *lowered* the release altitude angles as the threat from radar-guided SAMs and AAA forced aircraft further down. 'Gravity bombing' as a term bore little relation to the high-speed, air-frame-straining moments entailed in these manoeuvres! And they have changed little since: all that differs are the computers which do the 'thinking' for the crewmen, and the weapons themselves, which are far more controllable in terms of both safety and yield. Today, Britain and the United States employ only four key types of nuclear gravity bomb, the Mk./B57, Mk./B61, Mk./B83 and WE177, which are available in a number of different submodels. Under supervised 'US Key', they also equip the armouries of NATO allies Belgium, Germany, Greece, Italy and Turkey.

'SILVER BULLETS'

At the sharp end of America's current stockpile of air-delivered thermonuclear weapons is the Sandia/DoE Mk./B61, nicknamed the 'Silver Bullet' in deference to its streamlined shape and natural metal finish, which is tipped with an ominous red-brown frangible aluminium nose cone. Users range from the big 'swinger', the B-1B Lancer, which is capable of holding up to two dozen of them in clusters of eight on a trio of CSRLs (Common Strategic Rotary Launchers), through to its tactical forebear the F-111E/F which, while on standby 'Victor Alert' duties in England, carried one on each inner wing pivot-pylon — 'Like Coors Lite beer, they don't slow you down'! Some 3,000 of them remain on active service with the USAF, having now completely displaced the Mk./B57s which until very recently were distributed to European and South Korean bases, alongside the 'bullets', on full-time alert.[2]

The Mk./B61 was innovative inasmuch as it introduced the supersonic 'Lay Down' and LADD (and digital equivalent Dual Bomb

Timer) profiles, by means of a 17ft-diameter nylon parachute bundled into the rear of its streamlined tail, which permitted the bomber to enter or exit the target area just above the treetops and rock crags (in keeping with the low-level antics of the F-111 'Vark' which introduced it to operational service and, later, the tri-national Tornado). Money was lavished on the programme, with the result that the weapon developed its own 'cult' status within the USAF and gave rise to many jocular nicknames for the weapon and the nuclear assignment, all intended to bring a little light humour to this most serious business. SAC Mk./B61 pioneers the 509th BW(M) *Enola Gay* at Pease AFB, New Hampshire, christened their FB-111As the 'Bullet Bomber' in deference to the weapons it sported, while a decade later Capt. Ken Holder of the 492nd TFS *Bolars* scratched out the design of the memorable 'Warsaw Pact Central Heating' (alias 'Warming the Homes in Winter') logo, which spread quickly throughout the USAFE 'Vark' community and later through SAC, creating a host of patches, plaques, ashtrays, mugs and glasses festooned with the famous whirlwind 'mushroom' design.

Because of its low-drag configuration at release, the weapon is apt to stay close to its mothercraft until persuaded to separate from the bomber's slipstream, accomplished by means of a drogue 'chute which, at speed, must bear a force of up to 200 tons! Reliability here is crucial, lest the bomber get shredded in the shock and blast of its own weapon. Minimum delivery speed is 520kt. Beginning with the Mod. 3 version which entered production in June 1977, a new 24ft diameter Kevlar drogue 'chute was fitted as standard equipment, permitting 'Lay Downs' at altitudes ranging from 50ft to 5,000ft, at speeds in excess of Mach 2. Remarkably, even at these tremendous velocities, 200ft CEPs are commonly demonstrated during special Weapons Training Detachment (WTD) deployments—a negligible 'miss' distance given the selectable yield of 10–500 kilotons[3]. The 115lb drogue pack is forcibly evicted at 155fs from its snug compartment 0.3, 0.6 or 1.5 seconds after bomb release (adjustable according to bomb release altitude) by means of a gas-powered telescopic tube, which 'pumps iron' in proportion to its task.[4]

Development of this series began in Janu-ary 1963, with the 'standard' Mod. 0. This featured Category B PAL (Permissive Action Link) by means of a four-digit switch so that it could be armed, and the yield selected via a dial, from the cockpit. Six-digit (Cat D PAL) and 12-digit (Cat F PAL) Mk./B61 Mods. 2–5 followed it in series production between June 1975 and September 1979, alongside the strategic-only Mod. 1, all of which have undergone updates to Mod. 6–8 format, embracing the new Kevlar drogue 'chute and in-flight selectable FUFO (full-fuzing option) for arming in the 'slick' or retarded, air or surface burst modes. The former options depend on the delivery profile, i.e., clean aerodynamics for 'Lofting' versus drogue-assisted parabraking for LADD and 'Lay Down' deliveries. The latter are chosen according to the target to hand: a sprawling one, for example a factory or airfield, is better destroyed by an air burst; a nuclear missile silo or command and control bunker, buried deep underground, can only be effectively neutralized by a surface burst. Britain's WE177 works on almost identical principles. Unfortunately, no further details are in the public domain. Development details regarding the Tiger, a Mk./B61 propelled by a surplus Genie missile rocket motor, also remains under heavy wraps, though it is understood that the project has now been shelved completely following Stage Two of the Bush-Yeltsin nuclear climb-down.

Backing the 'bullets' are the dwindling numbers of strategic-only 'H-bombs'—the Mk./B53 and Mk./B83. The Mk./B53 remains exclusive to the B-52H, based on the W53 warhead used in the LGM-25C Titan II intercontinental missile, and was recalled into service for use against deeply buried Soviet command and control complexes and submarine pens—the nuclear counterpart to the tactical BLU-109/B. As such, it is intended to be dropped in 'Lay Down' drogue deliveries (delayed surface burst) or from high-altitude level flight (when the switches are set for immediate contact surface burst). It is the last remaining thermonuclear heavyweight, grossing in at 8,850lb and possessing a yield of 9 megatons. The Mk./B83 is fundamentally a bigger replacement for the Mk./B61 Mod. 1 for use by SAC, designed to fill the void left by the cancellation of the Mk./B77. It entered production in 1981 and stocks have been estimated at 1,000, optimized for ground burst against enemy bunkers and missile

► American nuclear bombers and crews conduct practice loadings with concrete-filled 'training shapes'. For full-sized drops, the air crews employ such simulators as the glossy white Douglas BDU-38/B and -46/B (depicted), which behave just like the 'heavy metal' Mk./B61 and Mk./B83, respectively, complete with their optional Kevlar retarding parachutes. (USAF)

US NUCLEAR WEAPONS

Designation	All-up weight (lb)	Yield	Production	Introduction	Inventory	Training shape
B43 Mod. 0–1	2,060–2,120	1 megaton	1959–70	IOC 1961	Out of inventory	–
B53	8,850	9 megatons	?	IOC 1960s	Small; B-52H only	BDU-12/B
B57 Mod. 0–1	500–510	Variable, 5–20 kilotons	1963–70	IOC 1964	1,000; under phase-out	BDU-12/B
B61 Mod. 0–4	718–765	Variable, 10 kilotons– 0.5 megaton	1967–87	IOC 1968	3,000+	BDU-38/B
B83	2,408	Variable, 1–2 megatons	1981–	IOC 1984	1,000+	BDU-46/B

silos with a yield in the 1–2mT range. A quadruple drogue 'chute arrangement has replaced the solitary system installed originally, and with periodic safety updates this bomb will be the last freefall nuclear device to be created in the West.

Training with these weapons of last resort is clearly out of the question, unlike conventional bombing where crews are given the opportunity to pound the ranges with the full-sized items and their concrete-filled Bomb, Dummy Munitions/Unit (BDM/BDU) equivalents. Electronic bomb-scoring by means of interrogating the bomber's Bomb-Nav-System and scrutinizing post-mission radarscope photography and video tape are the most frequently used alternatives, along with drops of innocuous 'training shapes' which emulate the characteristics of the live, heavy metal. For the US forces, these comprise three widely used dummy bombs. The BDU-48/B 'Beer Can' (known to US Navy/Marine crews as the Mk. 106), is a fat, dayglo-orange 10lb practice bomb which can be carried on specially adapted MERs and TERs, or more commonly on the widely used SUU-20/A or -21/A dispensers. Its ballistic properties closely resemble those of retarded nuclear weapons, but its destructive power is at the other end of the spectrum! When 'Tossed' and 'Lay-Down'-delivered against the concentrically-ringed target

ranges dotted around the outbacks of the Western US and Southern Europe, their small charge acts as a perfect indicator of the relevant crew's bombing prowess. Bigger and more realistic practice bombs come in the form of the giant glossy white BDU-38/D and BDU-46/B 'shapes', identical in most respects to their deadly cousins the Mk./B61 and Mk./B83 respectively, with stowed 'slick' and Kevlar chute-retarded delivery options but filled only with harmless concrete ballast to simulate handling of the live versions. These can be flung at the ranges during special WTDs, whilst also providing the armourers with experience of hauling the heavyweights about the flight-lines and up and down from the wings of their charges from the 'scoop' cradles of the standard MHU-83 'Jammers'—a diesel device handled with uncharacteristic trepidation by the tough support troops!

CRUISING

Gravity bombs such as the Mk./B61 and Mk./B83 are customarily employed against the 'primary' targets, deep in enemy territory. En route, nuclear bombers must first 'roll back' the enemy's defences, taking out the heavy concentrations of communications centres, radar and SAM networks that would present a series of challenges to the crews as they ambled on guard through enemy-controlled airspace: there is no time or leeway to mess about with ARMs or to get huge 'packages' to open up corridors. In similar vein, the heavier, more vulnerable dedicated bombers such as the aged B-52H 'Buff' require stand-off weapons so that they can punch their targets 'from arm's length', one, two or three at a time.

First in the series was the rocket-powered GAM-63A Rascal, achieving IOC at Eglin on 30 October 1957, followed by the GAM-77A/B (later designated the AGM-28A/B) Hound Dog, a J52 turbojet-powered air-breathing missile which was declared mission-ready four years later. This possessed an extended range of 710 miles in the hi-hi mission profile and represented one of the first true 'interfaced' systems available to SAC. Its jet engines could supplement the bank of eight fitted to the B-52G to assist with rapid climb to cruise altitude, after which time its tanks would be topped up from the bomber's fuel reserves just prior to release. By the early 1970s this had given way to the Boeing AGM-69A SRAM-A (Short-Range Attack Missile), packing a 200kT W69 warhead in a slender 2,230lb, 14ft-long airframe which could be carried in the 'Buff' in 'revolver packs' of eight at a time internally, and externally with the option of an aerodynamic tail cone, for a total of twenty rounds. Even the diminutive 'Bullet Bomber' could manage six at a go. SRAM possessed a modest maximum range of 105 miles, fired by a twin-stage XSR-75-LP-1 solid rocket motor, but, possessing the radar signature of a large bullet slug, was difficult for the enemy to detect. And it was 'smart'. Equipped with a Delco computer and a Singer-Kearfott KT-76 inertial measurement unit, it could be 'fed' with a 'navigation model' by the bomber's Offensive Systems Officer and launched in

▶ The first operational long-range, air-breathing strategic missile was the North American Rockwell GAM-77 (later AGM-28) Hound Dog, a 42ft-long craft powered by a P&WA J52 turbojet and possessing a range of 710 miles. It could be used to supplement the 'Duff's' engines on take-off, and then topped up with fuel from the bomber's tanks just prior to release. Initial deliveries equipped the B-52Gs of the 4135th Strategic Wing at Eglin AFB, Florida, beginning on 21 December 1959. The unit conducted its first operational Category III test launch on 29 February 1960 following a non-stop flight to the Arctic and back, appropriately titled Operation 'Blue Nose'. (Boeing)

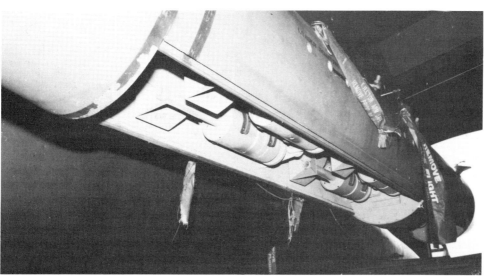

◀ This cylindrical 'Soo-Twenty-One' (SUU-21), equipped with twin compartments and bay doors, has been employed since the 1960s by American fighters stationed in Europe and the Pacific. It was photographed fitted with six dayglo-orange BDU-48 (Mk. 106) 5lb high-drag practice bombs, which behave very much like a parachute-retarded Mk./B61. (Author)

four different modes: 'inertial', wherein the missile was launched at a set altitude and bearing to the target for optimum accuracy; 'terrain sensor', in which SRAM employed a radar altimeter to skim over the topography to avoid detection; 'combined' inertial and terrain-following; and 'semi-ballistic', in which the weapon was lobbed at the target in a Mach 3 ballistic rocket trajectory, when range counted for more than pinpoint accuracy. So clever was it that aircraft with 'down' Bomb-Nav-Systems frequently used the missile for their own guidance! Produc-

tion had reached 1,500 rounds by the time the line closed in July 1975, at which point it was sitting ready for action with the alert bomber forces at eighteen SAC bases. First in the league was the B-52G-equipped 42nd Bomb Wing at Loring AFB, Maine, which received its first operational missiles on 4 March 1972. The *Aethera Nobis* fired their first round (equipped with an inert warhead) a short while later, on 15 June, over the restricted grounds of the White Sands Missile Range in New Mexico. After a successful eighteen-year career stretching to 7 June

▶ A SAC FB-111A test-bed makes a change of heading with polka-dotted test SRAM-As during Category II trials. The interface between the aircraft's bomb-nav system and the weapons' Singer-Kearfott inertial reference system was substantial, so that the weapons began 'thinking' about their target destination well before launch. Operational tests were conducted under Project 'Bullet Blitz'. By 1975, SAC had acquired 1,500 rounds, and these remained on full-time alert for a further fifteen years. (USAF)

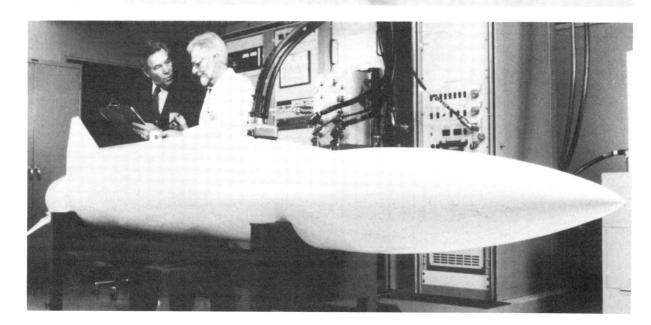

1990, by which time some 300 inert missiles had been expended in training, it was withdrawn from use in wholesale fashion under the express orders of Defense Secretary Richard B. Cheney. Apparently, experts expressed concern regarding the close proximity of the weapon's rocket motor to its nuclear warhead, which could present a significant hazard in the event of a fire: commensurate with the slackening of international tensions, more attention has been devoted to safety considerations. The weapon's intended successors, the Boeing SRAM-2 and tactical nuclear SRAM-T, were cancelled in September 1991 as part of continuing cutbacks to the strategic arsenal. The USAF is now casting around for a substitute.

In the meantime, work had recently been completed on the ultimate air-launched missile: the air-to-space Vought anti-satellite ASAT. If a nuclear exchange were to take place, satellites—responsible for reconnaissance, targeting, post-strike damage assessment, communications and navigation aids—would be primary targets. Measuring 17ft long and fitted with a redundant AGM-69A rocket booster mated to a classified fragmentation warhead, ASAT had a simple job: launched from altitude from an F-15 Eagle, it would zoom on a collision course with enemy communications or spy satellites and then pepper the fragile celestial orbiter with shrapnel. In the era of East–West détente, when even the 'Star Wars' programme itself is beginning to be questioned,

the ASAT has been shelved; but the technology remains there to be resurrected, if needed. Certainly, copious stocks of SRAM boosters have been available ever since the AGM-69A was taken off alert.

On the other side of the Atlantic, and very much alive and well, is France's ASMP (Air-Sol Moyenne Portée), a 300km (186-mile) range missile powered by a combined solid-propellant booster backed by a ramjet sustainer. It is built by SNI Aérospatiale and packs a CEA 150kT warhead. Its existing design was initiated in 1978, and it went on to achieve IOC with the Mirage IVAs of the Armée de l'Air Force de Frappe in 1986. Featuring hi- or lo-launch capability, it is also now operational with the Mirage 2000N, and with the Super Etendards of the Aéronavale, supplementing the small-yield CEA AN-22 and -52 freefall gravity bombs employed by both services. Although periodic updates continue, Aérospatiale has switched attention to the follow-on long-ranged ASLP (Air-Sol Longue Portée), powered by an integral rocket/ramjet which will offer 'several times the range' of the ASMP, and it is intended that this be deployed at the turn of the century aboard land- and sea-based versions of the new Rafale combat aircraft.

Britain, devoid of a stand-off nuclear missile since the progressive phase-out of the 'Blue Steel' between 1973 and 1975, has, for the last five years, under the auspices of BAe, been developing a 125nm-range glide weapon.[5] Designed for conventional work in

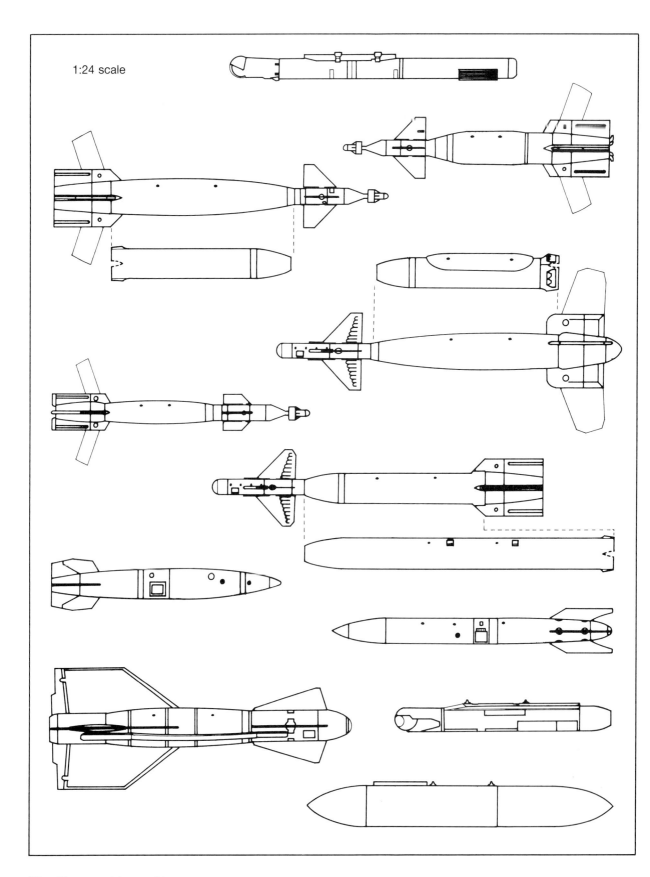

1:24 scale

two key formats—the MANTIS (Man-in-the-loop Target Interdiction System), which features a tandem 400kg (881.8lb) warhead for use against hardened targets, and the REVISE (Research Vehicle for In-Flight Sub-munition Ejection), which is packed with sub-munitions—the weapon is scheduled to grow into the 324nm-range Autonomous Target Interdiction System (AUTIS) with the capability of delivering a nuclear warhead. Guidance for the baseline MANTIS version, under development by GEC Avionics, is based on microwave data link for arm's-length guidance by means of a dual-imaging TV and infra-red seeker. Further details remain sketchy, though flight tests have been in progress for some time in the custody of RAF Boscombe Down's 'Raspberry Ripple' Tornado GR.1 (ZA326). The programme's successful outcome is heavily dependent upon whether the Ministry of Defence continues to fund the system through the fiscal ups-and-downs of the 'Options for Change' policy or purchases the new American range of TSSAMs.

The 'luxury' models of the nuclear missile series are the air-breathers, technically known as ALCMs (Air Launched Cruise Missiles) but more often referred to by the evocative name 'Cruise'—the mention of which causes US aviators to tighten their lips and peace protestors to shout and rave. ALCMs owe their origins to studies into decoys at the height of the 'nuclear age', designed for endurance and packing state-of-the-art countermeasures, with a view towards emulating the characteristics of the launch aircraft and, in some cases, backing up the decoy emissions with a nuclear warhead to boot—the ultimate distraction! This philosophy began its operational life in February 1960 as the Douglas ADM-20A Quail, a box-like, 1,100lb, fibreglass active decoy, up to two of which could be released from the belly of a 'Buff'. After release it would pop out its winglets, permitting it to cruise for up to half an hour by means of a kerosene-fed GE J85 turbojet.[6] It remained operational until 1978, at which point tests of a worthy successor were well underway. Starting life as the Boeing SCAD (Subsonic Cruise Armed Decoy), this soon evolved into a fully fledged nuclear air-breathing missile using an IMU/radar altimeter navigation system similar to that of SRAM but possessing a range of 745 miles. It was test-flown as the AGM-86A from 5

March 1976 (the SCAD test-beds distinguished by their sharkmouths!) but it soon was realized that this decoy-cum-weapon could be developed further into a dedicated 'cruise' missile with double the range of the original model—and capable of staggering precision when matched with Tercom (terrain-commanded) guidance. The subsequent AGM-86B was essentially a 'stretch' from 14ft to 19½ft, doubling fuel capacity. Development was given the go-ahead by President Jimmy Carter concurrent with his cancellation of the B-1A programme. Commensurate miniaturization in the guidance systems as microchip technology came to the fore also enabled the designers to maximize Tercom (known generically as TRN or terrain-referenced navigation). The ALCM concept was thrown open to competition between the AGM-86B and GD's AGM-109A during 1979.

While the US Navy/GD AGM-109A went on to be perfected as the hugely successful ground-, ship- and submarine-launched BGM-109 Tomahawk series, Boeing won the contract to develop its AGM-86B specifically for SAC's big bombers, giving the by then seemingly antediluvian but much-respected 'Buff' some desperately needed stand-off clout.[7] IOC was achieved during 1981 aboard the B-52G, with production reaching 1,715 rounds adapted to the Mk.2 Boeing CSRL, which has recently ousted the old SRAM 'revolver'. TRN, the 'brains' of the system, deserves further discussion, especially as the technology is creeping into the world of conventional munitions guidance. Essentially, the system works by comparing radar altimeter (height above ground level) and barometric (height above sea level) pressure to deduce both missile altitude and the elevation of the terrain below; these electronic notes are then compared with the position stored in its IMU (the latest of which feature a laser disc from which can be accessed up to four million square miles of terrain, based on the Defense Mapping Agency's digital land mass files—in essence, digital contour maps). By this cross-reference process, the missile can deduce exactly where it is, enabling it to maintain a safe terrain-avoidance profile throughout the navigation attack profile. CEPs were stated to be 'in the order of 100ft'—trifling for a nuclear warhead. However, these figures were in fact bettered by 35 conventionally tipped examples (specially reconfigured for 'Desert Storm' operations), which were launched from seven B-52Gs from the 2nd BW *Libertatem Defendimus* against critical targets dotted around Mosul in Northern Iraq during the opening stages of the air campaign. The crews launched their weapons fifty miles from the Saudi Arabian border following a gruelling 34hr 20min non-stop mission from Barksdale AFB, Louisiana. Until the Turkish authorities permitted operations by the 4770th Combat Wing from Icirlik AB, these were the only aircraft capable of striking that far into enemy territory without the need to send aerial refuelling tankers into enemy airspace.

The all-up nuclear AGM-86B model currently serves with all of SAC's nuclear-committed 'Buffs'. There remains only one source of concern: the enemy's ability to shoot these down as they ply their obedient track at low

◀ Boeing AGM-86B Air Launched Cruise Missiles undergo flight-line check-out at Griffis AFB, New York. This air-breathing nuclear weapon uses terrain-referenced navigation techniques and forms the primary nuclear deterrent of America's still sizeable B-52H force. The weapons were taken off full-time alert, along with the 'Buffs' of Strategic Air Command, on the express orders of President George Bush on the morning of 28 September 1991. Although the missiles seen in these two photographs are dummies, the white 'drum' is the business end of ALCM, its W80-1 nuclear warhead. The entire arrangement, ALCMs and pylon, 'costs as much, weighs as much and is as complex as an early model F-16 fighter', according to the Air Force. (Boeing)

▲ Northrop's 'Strategic Boomerang' is designed to carry a formidable weapons load in three bays. It is intended that the bombers enter operational service with the USAF Combat Command at Whiteman AFB, Missouri, in 1994, for long-ranged nuclear and conventional attack. A typical strategic configuration will be two Common Strategic Rotary Launcher 'revolver' loads each of eight B83 gravity bombs for a 4,400nm unrefuelled hi-lo-hi mission profile, jumping to 6,600nm if lighter B61s are employed. (USAF)

level. Their BGM-109 counterparts soaring over Baghdad could be 'caged' by TV news cameramen, while a percentage must have formed part of the Iraqi claims of 'hundreds of enemy aircraft shot down', despite the numerous Chukar drones and TALD decoys which simply 'ran out of gas and crashed', having already accomplished their tasks.

Not surprisingly, 'stealth' has now become the byword of the embryonic 'Air Combat Command', which is enjoying access to 'invisible' ALCMs. Spreading their copious weight on eight tyres, the nuclear 'Buffs' are now being fitted with the GD AGM-129A Advanced Cruise Missile. Spawned from the A/BGM-109 series but given a new angular, stealthy look and topcoat of RAM (radar-absorbent material), 640 of these are on the inventory. Fitted with the same W80 thermonuclear warheads as their forebears (some of them removed from redundant BGM-109 GLCMs or poached from aged AGM-86B stock), the 'cruisers' have simply

been 'revisited' with low observability in mind. Tercom is also being supplemented with added extras which permit target co-ordinate updates via satellite, to cater for strikes against mobile facilities such as rail-based ICBMs. This programme, along with the fledgeling TSSAM, is becoming gradually 'blacker'.

Quite what the future holds, given the reduced impetus for producing new weapons of mass destruction, remains to be seen. 'Deterrence' holds little credence with the peace-seeking Commonwealth of Independent States, the fragmented former Soviet Union, which has far too many domestic troubles to concern itself with, yet far more so with the burgeoning arms-conscious nations of the Middle and Near East. However, by virtue of their 'Third World' status, these are off-limits to nuclear attack except in the *direst* of circumstances. Indeed, although the use of 'nukes' in 'brushfire wars' has been mooted since V-J Day in the Pacific—Korea, Vietnam and, indeed, the Gulf, prompted discussion of specific retaliatory measures using these last-resort weapons (which were stationed at several bases close to the heart of Operation 'Desert Storm')—their employment has never progressed beyond the hypotheses of the planning stages. It also appears that nuclear weapons are becoming militarily as well as politically obsolete. As American Chief of Staff Gen. Colin Powell ably summarized, and as one USAF officer reiterated, 'In anything short of a general war, or need for a nuclear retaliation, conventional PGMs are *as capable* at target destruction, and much less controversial'. The art of aerial warfare is once again in rapid flux.

NOTES TO CHAPTER FOUR

1. SAC dropped its first *air-transportable* hydrogen bomb on 21 May 1956, from a Boeing B-52B flying at 50,000ft over Bikini Atoll in the Pacific Ocean. Shortly afterwards, the more compact weapons began to equip all of SAC's bombers, including RB-36 recce aircraft, and to percolate down into the inventories of sea-going and land-based tactical fighter-bombers (see below). Britain's first atomic bomb was dropped on 11 October 1956 over Maralinga, Southern Australia, by Vickers Valiant WZ366 of No. 49 Squadron, captained by Sqn. Ldr. E. J. G. Flavell, and its first hydrogen bomb over the Pacific in the Christmas Island area on 15 May 1957, by another No. 49 Squadron Valiant, crewed by Wg. Cdr. K. G. Hubbard. France joined the league a decade later and quit NATO to pursue its own efforts without hindrance from the United States and Britain. The declared possession of nuclear weapons gives members rights to a prestigious seat on the United Nations Permanent Security Council.

2. The bulk of the obsolescent arsenal is held under wraps in spick-and-span storage at Minot AFB, South Dakota, with pockets of the weapons distributed throughout the relevant operational installations. B57s and B61s remained on 'Victor Alert' with USAFE F-4D/Es and F-111E/Fs until superseded by truck-transportable Tomahawk BGM-109 Ground Launched Cruise Missiles during 1984, a mission which was not resumed following the removal of 'Cruise'. Of the US Navy inventory of 1,000 such weapons, 400 of the sea-going B57s (bombs and depth charges) and B61s (bombs only) were removed from the Fleet and placed in storage as and when the ships docked for resupply, at the earliest date following the Bush Directive of 27 September 1991. Up to that time they were earmarked for carriage principally aboard land-based P-3C Orions and carrier-assigned S-3A/B Vikings and A-6E Intruders. As of October 1991, only US Navy Trident 1/C4 and 2/D5 submarine-launched missiles remained on alert. Interestingly, Japan still forbids US Navy ships suspected of carrying nuclear weapons rights of entry to her ports. All American nuclear devices were recently removed from South Korea to help promote the new North–South nuclear-free zone peace initiatives.

3. Hence the crews' satisfaction when hitting target ranges with this degree of accuracy, a process usually conducted with little 'Beer Can' Mk. 106/BDU-48 practice bombs. See below.

(These miniature practice munitions also replicate the characteristics of retarded 'iron' bombs such as the Mk. 82 Snakeye and Mk. 80 series Ballutes). Bombing accuracy in these circumstances is significantly less important than practising the delivery profile itself and *timing*.

4. Its 'beef' matches the job at hand. In one instance, while fitted to FB-111A 68-259 on the ramp at Nellis AFB prior to a 1981 'Red Flag' mission, a BDU-38/B training version of the Mk./B61 was inadvertently activated and its telescope, pack and tail cone smashed straight through the forged steel bulkheads of the aircraft's weapons bay, ending up as a messy ensemble in the already cramped maingear compartment. The aircraft had to be dispatched to its manufacturers at Fort Worth, Texas, for major repairs, having been taken off flight status in the process; multiple failures of this variety would cause the aft end of a B-1B to pop off like a champagne cork! Safety reviews are constant and thorough.

5. 'Blue Steel' was a Mach Two missile capable of flying its attack navigation profile at altitudes ranging from 'low-level up to 80,000ft'. Production-standard rounds of the hefty 34ft 9in long weapons were tested at Woomera, Australia, during 1959, and the systems achieved IOC with the Vulcan B.2s of No. 617 Squadron ('The Dam-Busters') in June 1962. The weapon also went on to equip the Vulcans of Nos. 27 and 83 Squadrons and the Victor B.2s of Nos. 139 and 100 Squadrons, in that order. Recessed in conformal carriage mode into the belly of the Vulcan and Victor (which lent the latter its bulbous-nosed and recessed ventral aerodynamics), the weapon remained on standby until replaced completely by the submarine-carried Polaris.

6. The J85 turbojet became the powerplant of the Northrop T-38/F-5 and Cessna A/37 'families'. The similarly reliable J52 of the AGM-28 Hound Dog, described earlier, also became the standard engine for the US Navy's Douglas A-4 and A-6 series.

7. In its conventional format, the US Navy/GD BGM-109 was one of the first weapons to be launched during 'Desert Storm'. It is available in nuclear-tipped and conventionally armed formats which feature blast and fragmentation warheads, in the 'Alpha' to 'Golf' variants, all of which use similar Tercom guidance to the AGM-86B described below.

5.
THE BATTLE OF THE BEAMS

GETTING TO the target and then success- fully deploying PGMs and even 'iron' bombs is heavily dependent on the skilful use of related navigation and targeting aids, which ultimately either 'sparkle' the quarry for them to home on to, using their superior resolution imagery to acquire them to begin with before 'handing them off' to the weapons, or perform the simple but essential task of computing automatic weapons release during 'uncanned' attack profiles. Moreover, amidst the murky skies of Europe and the Pacific or the dust-bowl of the desert, any device which can shave a few seconds off the target acquisition process is a boon to an aircrew's longevity! The old say- ing 'Speed is Life' is one adage which remains as true today as it was in the trail- blazing era of piston-propelled air power.

When the Gulf War burst upon the world, perhaps the most popularized airborne aids were the laser 'guns' and their related electro-optic sensors, the imagery from which made good news bulletin material when accompanied by typically inane media narrative which coined such memorable phrases as 'chillingly precise', and 'doomed to inevitable destruction'. The reporters spoke of these systems as if they had evolved only yesterday, yet their origins can be traced to the mid-1960s and the protrac- ted war in South-East Asia.[1]

LASER GUNS
The great pioneer was the Martin Marietta AVQ-9/9A Paveway ALD (Airborne Laser Designator), developed in partnership with Texas Instruments which produced the actual Paveway laser guidance 'groups' for the M117/118 and Mk. 80 series munitions. Fielded in the summer of 1968, Paveway comprised a hefty 'pack' which was carried out to the flight-lines by the navigators of the

élite F-4D-equipped 8th TFW *Wolfpack* based at Ubon, Thailand, clipped on to the right-hand rear canopy rail and simply plug- ged into the aircraft's power supply ready for the mission. Once over the 'fragged' target co-ordinates, the pilot entered into a pylon turn at a slant range of anything up to 20,000ft, while the 'Wizzo' looked into a tele- scopic viewfinder, acquired the target in the crosshairs and 'sparkled' it with the YAG laser 'gun', making minor corrections by means of a pistol grip at the base of the 'pack'. 'Buddy' bombers would then lob their KMU 'smart' bombs into the reflected 'laser basket'. It was simple and extremely effi- cient, and earned the specialist Phantom crews the nickname 'Zot', after the anteater in the *BC* cartoon strip. By war's end the fourteen Paveway 'guns' had guided 14,301 LGBs to target, with a mission reliability of 99.7 per cent.

By 1972, the philosophy had been refined into the Ford Aerospace (now Loral Aero- nutronic) AN/AVQ-10 Pave Knife, a 1,200lb banana-shaped pod which featured a neodymium YAG laser gun boresighted with a Low Light-Level Television (LLLTV) camera which amplified available light to generate a TV picture in the cockpit, flashed up on a small 5in Sony tube. This permitted the 'pit- ter' in the F-4D Phantom, or right-seater in the A-6A Intruder, to manoeuvre the sensor head until the target appeared in the display crosshairs. With the LGBs drifting to earth as planned, the navigator then 'lased' the target, as before. It offered many advantages over its pioneering predecessor. The steerable sensor head covered the entire lower hemi- sphere beneath the aircraft, not just a limited quadrant to the side, and could also be boresighted with the pilot's gunsight for 'Forward Acquire' in visual conditions, to put the sensor on target, overcoming the diffi-

culties of initial acquisition. Moreover, it introduced the concept of autonomous 'smart' bombing—i.e., the same aircraft dropping and designating. Pave Knife met with considerable success once its crews had grown accustomed to its vices. Six of twelve Pave Knife 'Rhinos' converted to the task and assigned to the 433rd TFS *Satan's Angels* dropped bridge after bridge between 6 April and 30 June 1972 before graduating on to point targets in Hanoi (all previously off-limits because of fears of collateral damage from 'dumb' bombs) later in the year.[2] It also saw action with the US Navy. Three Intruders from VA-145 *Swordsmen* assigned to the USS *Ranger* were outfitted with Pave Knife during their pre-cruise exercises at MCAS El Toro, California, and during their WESTPAC Line Periods with Task Force 77 between September 1972 and June 1973 successfully guided 54 Paveway I bombs on to lucrative targets dotted around the inner sanctuaries of Haiphong and buried in the lush vegetation and tertiary limestone topography of Cambodia with equally convincing results.

In typical go-it-alone fashion, the US Navy were also busy at work developing their own laser-bombing system as an offshoot of the experimental Trails, Roads Interdiction

Multisensor (TRIM), designed to help attack the elusive Vietnamese convoys of supply trucks which snaked through Laos along the Ho Chi Minh Trail. TRIM was first flown in combat in 1967 on board specially modified AP-2H Neptunes based at Cam Ranh Bay, South Vietnam, during the opening stages of the 'Commando Hunt' assault on the Trail and by 1970 had been adapted into a hefty cupola bolted to a dozen specially built A-6C Intruders, integrated with the 'Iron Tadpole's' DIANE (Digitally Integrated Attack and Navigation Equipment). A-6Cs went on line over the South China Sea from 26 May 1970 with Cdr. Zick's VA-165 *Boomers*, flying from the deck of the USS *America*. In this early format the TRIM employed an LLLTV, together with a night-time FLIR sensor which picked up hot-on-cold or cold-on-hot contrast to generate a false image of the world outside the cockpit.[3] The harnessing of this technology would in the long term have as much of an impact as radar did in the 1940s. Once activated, the imagery from either of the two sensors was displayed in the cockpit on a new 'IARM' tube, to supplement the radar sector-scan mapper which had difficulty picking up non-radar-significant targets (such as headquarters, or roaming trucks)

▲ The Loral Aeronutronic AN/AVQ-10A Pave Knife targeting pod was the forerunner to some of today's most advanced E-O acquisition and lasing systems. It was used by F-4D Phantoms of the 433rd TFS *Satan's Angels* based at Ubon, Thailand, and by A-6A Intruders of the US Seventh Fleet's VA-145 *Swordsmen*. This Intruder, Modex 504, assigned to Lt. Cdr. J. J. Juan for ATKRON One-Four-Five's seven-month WESTPAC aboard the USS *Ranger*, was one of three aircraft so configured for the cruise. (Loral)

▲ First to receive the Westinghouse AN/ASQ-153 Pave Spike were the USAF LORAN 'Towel Bar' F-4Ds, stationed at Kunsan in South Korea and Spangdahlem, Germany. A knight-like visor shields the optics in the steerable seeker head. The pod carries the designation AN/AVQ-23 when not integrated with the Phantom's WRCS (Weapons Release Computer System). (Author)

owing to their poor radar signature, a situation exacerbated by the cloak of the tropical rain forest. Cued initially by DIANE's inertial navigation system (from a well-known offset aiming point—a feature readily recognizable on radar) to put the aircraft in the vicinity of the target's co-ordinates, the sensors would then be employed to identify it positively. With the radars slaved to the sensors to provide ranging data for the ballistics computer, the navigator would then 'commit' the system to attack and leave the computers to handle weapon release. In this early format TRIM was thus a grandiose sensor package designed to assist with radar 'blind bombing' and navigation by night, permitting crews to see 'out of the windshield' for the first time ever, without the use of flares or bright moonlight which would otherwise betray their presence to enemy AAA.

By August 1972 TRIM had been revised with an updated FLIR and the LLLTV had been discarded in favour of the much-coveted laser gun. Assigned to the VA-35 *Black Panthers* for WESTPAC duties, the system demonstrated the same degree of pinpoint accuracy as that shown by the USAF 'Knifers' (albeit exclusively as a 'buddy', owing to the physical tracking limi-

tations of the TRIM turret), and lent new meaning to the term 'night time capability'. 'Smart' munitions and their all-important target markers had come of age, thanks largely to zealous American inter-service rivalries, although the world would not know of their existence for another two decades.

In the very short term, and following close on the heels of Pave Knife, came the Westinghouse Pave Spike, of which some 156 were acquired for the USAF F-4 fleet between 1974 and 1979, including many of its FMS customers. The chief advantages of this pod were its aerodynamically slender design (fitted to a low drag adapter under the Sparrow missile well of the Phantoms) and its advanced features. First, it overcame the limitations of the steerable Pave Knife, which, according to 'zotter' Capt. Harry Edwards, 'caused what we saw in the rear cockpit to appear upside down and backwards!' This was achieved by means of image autorotation, to compensate for the aircraft's movement as it passed by or over the target, so that the imagery always appeared the right way up (or 'horizon natural')—a simple modification, but one which invoked numerous technical complexities in the pre-microchip age. But the biggest feature of all was its

◄ The highly classified Trails, Interdiction Multisensor (TRIM) project was inaugurated during 1967 as a means of identifying elusive traffic in Laos. It was subsequently applied to a dozen A-6C Intruders as a cupola interfaced with the Intruder's DIANE nav-and-attack system. The first such aircraft saw action with VA-165 *Boomers* aboard the USS *America* between May and November 1970, during which time 675 A-6C sorties were flown. Equipped, to begin with, with a FLIR and LLLTV, in 1972 the aircraft had the latter sensor replaced with a laser to adapt them for 'smart buddy' bombing duties with VA-35 *Black Panthers*. (Grumman Archives)

ability to help deliver 'dumb' bombs more accurately as well as guide laser PGMs, a feat made possible by integrating the laser receiver with the Phantom's automatic WRCS (Weapons Release Computer System), by picking-up the coded, tiny-wavelength, pulsed reflections to provide extremely accurate laser slant-range measurements to target. This ranging information was used in lieu of radar to help calculate optimum automatic 'bombs away', and effectively halved CEPs. With due deference to its number-crunching functions, Pave Spike was bestowed with the title AN/ASQ-153, using the airborne 'special type' prefix reserved for bombing computers. It remains in service with the FMS Phantoms of Israel and Turkey to this day, and it has been embroiled in combat since 4 July 1976, when Pave Spike Phantoms flew as back-up strike cover during Operation 'Thunderbolt', the daring Israeli hostage extraction from Entebbe, Uganda. The latest 'Kurnass 2000' updated F-4Es retain the capability, as do the 'Rhinos' of the *Turk Hava Kuvvetleri*.

The mostly clear, blue skies of the Middle East have remained Pave Spike's primary venue, to which its daytime-only TV sensor is ideally suited. In its definitive AVQ-23E format (designator function only) it has lent the RAFs ageing Buccaneers 'a bit of smart'. Resplendent in their matt 'Desert Pink' liveries and later bestowed with 'Jolly Rogers', the names of Scotch whiskies and

some of the most tastefully erotic nose art to emerge during the war in the Persian Gulf, a dozen of these Spey-powered aircraft, operating out of Muharraq, Bahrain, flew 218 sorties, during which they guided a total of 169 CPU-123/B 1,000-pounders (121 in 'buddy' fashion and 48 autonomously). These bombs 'splashed' 24 bridges and spread carnage at fifteen airfields: typical tactics called for the Buccaneers to arrive at the target area in level flight and 'paint' them for the Tornados' bombs, before entering into a dive for the delivery of their own 'smart' munitions.[4] The AVQ-23E performed admirably for a twenty year-old system, as did the venerable 'Buccs' and their youthful

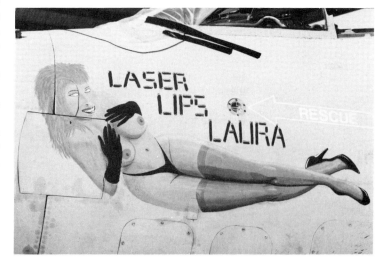

◄ AN/AVQ-23E Pave Spike optics on parade. Twelve RAF Buccaneer S.2s were assigned to Muharraq in Bahrain for 'buddy' and autonomous laser duties during 'Desert Storm', guiding Portsmouth Aviation CPU-123/B LGBs to target. (Author)

◄ 'Laser Lips Laura' was one of the more borderline examples of erotic nose art applied to RAF machines. The most tasteful — and professionally executed — were those applied to the Victor tanker force, which one Tornado pilot described as 'fit to fight in'. By contrast, some of the fighter aircraft artwork was a 'defacement of the aircraft with lavatory door-style humour'. (Bill Brookes Squadron Supplies)

occupants (who have the right to the curious claim that their aircraft boast laser guns as standard equipment but not INS!).

TRAM AND TACK

From the motley collection of Vietnam-era ALDs emerged two key second-generation packages which combined the best of all these devices — the follow-on to TRIM, the US Navy/Hughes AN/AAS-33 TRAM (Target Recognition and Attack, Multisensor), and the USAF/Loral Aeronutronic AN/AVQ-26 Pave Tack. Both of these combine an all-weather FLIR sensor with a laser gun and receiver, backed by an Airborne Video Tape Recorder (AVTR), interfaced with the aircraft's on-board attack radar sets: as the range to target closes, the navigators switch to the electro-optic sensors to ensure that the desired quarry is squarely in the cross-hairs.[5] Once this is accomplished, the lasers can be 'squirted' to 'sparkle' (the RAF uses the term 'paint') the target for LGBs or to provide laser slant-range measurements accurate to within inches, to assist the ballistic 'black boxes' in their arduous electronic task of continually computing the release point of unguided 'dumb' bombs. Until 10 November 1988, when the Department of Defense publicly acknowledged the existence of the Lockheed F-117A stealth fighter and its 'smart bombing' package, the TRAM Intruder's and the 'Tack Vark's' places at the top of league remained unchallenged.

The subsequent and inevitable rivalries between the three top-of-the-line 'smart' bombers, with Tornado joining in later, proved to be the spur for some remarkable all-round performances during Operation 'Desert Storm'!

The first A-6E Intruder equipped with TRAM joined the Fleet on 1 December 1978, and the system has since been retrofitted to, or installed-as-new in, all 320 machines still on the inventory. Manifesting itself as an innocuous 'thimble' protruding from the radome, and interfaced with the machine's radar bomb-nav set, it is the 'all-seeing eye' of the sea-going Intruder 'ATKRONS', endowing them with a 'bull's-eye' strike capability when employing LGBs, AGM-123A Skippers or AGM-65E/F Mavericks, as well as three times the 'dumb' bombing accuracy of the Vietnam-era A-6A. TRAM machines assigned to VA-35 on board the USS *Nimitz* remained on standby in support of Operation 'Eagle Claw', the aborted attempt to extract 66 American hostages from Teheran in April 1980, but had to wait another six years before finally proving their mettle, when President Reagan cast off their chains for Operation 'El Dorado Canyon', the punitive strike against Libya. On the night of 15 April 1986, fourteen A-6E TRAM Intruders from VA-34 *Blue Blasters* and VA-55 *Warhorses* catapulted from the decks of the USS *Coral Sea* and USS *America*, carrying clutches of Snakeyes and Rockeyes which were deposited on Benina military airfield and the Al Jumahiriyah barracks without loss to the attackers. TRAM proved its worth as both a targeting aid and a strike damage recorder. Oddly, LGBs were not used, a pattern which remained largely true during Operation 'Desert Storm' five years later. The Intruders were some of the busiest aircraft at sea, yet TRAMs laser guided only a modest 1,234 LGBs and Skippers, representing less than 10 per cent of such all ordnance expended by the US Navy—dispelling once for all time the myth that the laser systems are good only for guiding 'smart' bombs. TRAM also lived up to manufacturer Hughes' claims by picking out oil in storage holds, differentiating between dummy and live targets and so on—important capabilities which are impossible to accomplish with a fleeting glimpse with 'Mark One Eyeballs' or the beacon scan from a radar beam. In fact, TRAM permitted the combat squadrons to fly 80 per cent of their missions under the cloak of darkness, including the terribly dangerous but little publicized low-level mining operations conducted in the thick of Iraqi AAA defences at Umm Qafr. All this was carried out despite extensive 'optical counter-measures'. As Cdr. Denby Starling, skipper of VA-145 *Swordsmen* noted, 'Once they started torching the oil wells, every time you'd go out flying you'd come back with this film of gunk all over the airplane'. His squadron, along with the eight sister A-6E

TRAM units in the theatre, each generated an average of 620–630 combat sorties, forming the backbone of Navy tac-air and demonstrating a reliability rate of over 90 per cent. Systems like TRAM seem to be keeping the now thirty-year-old 'Iron Lady' endlessly youthful.[6]

The USAF, by contrast, has consistently employed PGMs to the full. The key exponents for over a decade have been the Pave Tack-equipped F-111Fs of the 48th TFW *Statue of Liberty Wing*, which received 86 of the 167 pods manufactured for the USAF and its overseas clients the RAAF and South Korea. The phallic shaped pod, adapted to fit a rotating weapons bay cradle in the

▼ The Loral Aeronutronic AN/AVQ-26A Pave Tack targeting pod may be strapped to the belly of ARN-101(V) DMAS (Digital Modular Avionics System)-updated Phantoms or nestle in the rotating belly cradle of the F-111C/F 'Tack Vark'. The Phantom fit is demonstrated here, clearly showing the pod's lines and the rear turret housing laser transmitter/receiver 'peep holes' and a large gallium arsenide FLIR 'window'. (Loral)

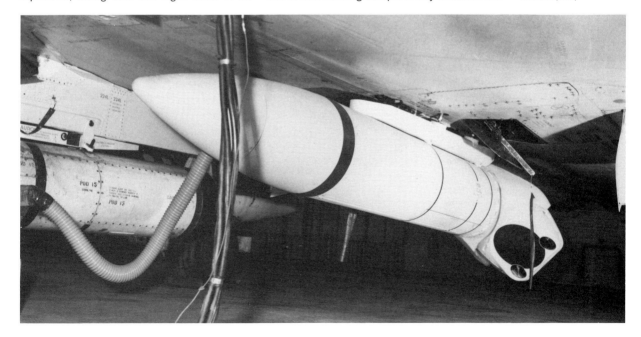

◄ The AN/AAS-33 Direction and Ranging Set 'thimble' mounted under the radome of an A-6. This device, known as the Target Recognition and Attack, Multisensor (TRAM), combines a laser gun with FLIR for round-the-clock precision bombing. (Author)

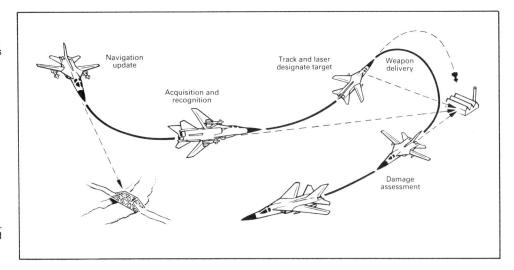

Navigation update

Acquisition and recognition

Track and laser designate target

Weapon delivery

Damage assessment

► Pave Tack navigation and 'Tack Toss' weapons delivery. Low-level F-15E LANTIRN and A-6E TRAM laser deliveries are similar in philosophy.

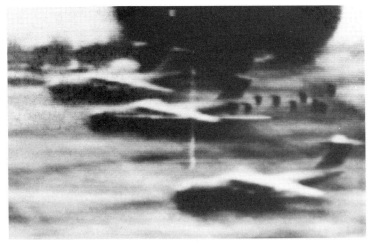

▲ Pave Tack imagery taken from an F-111F's airborne video tape recorder following Operation 'El Dorado Canyon', the strike against Libya. The black 'blobs' are Mk. 82 AIRs descending on the line-up of Il-76 'Candids'. (DoD)

F-111F for reduced drag and pod integrity, achieved IOC at the RAF Lakenheath, England, in September 1981, following an extensive work-up managed by the system Project Officer, Maj. Bob Rudiger.[7] In common with TRAM, the Pave Tack aviators introduced the system to combat during 'El Dorado Canyon' when thirteen 'Tack Varks' struck an underwater sabotage school at Sidi Bilal and bulldozed their way through the flak over Tripoli to strike Col. Qadaffi's infamous headquarters the Bab Al Azziziyah barracks, and to smash Tripoli Airport, using sextets of Mk. 82 AIRs and quartets of GBU-10 LGBs. Some criticisms were levelled at the reliability of the system. The strike was to be carried out by eighteen aircraft, but five aborted their bomb runs owing to 'down systems'. However, these difficulties mostly concerned the other systems (among them the F-111's radars and generator, and crew timing), not

the new electro-optics, and many have since been improved for both safety and reliability as a spin-off from the fleetwide Avionics Modernization Program.

Pave Tack's real success came in the Gulf, when sixty-six 'Tack Varks' of Col. Tom Lennon's 48th TFW(P) deployed to Taif, Saudi Arabia, to form the sharp edge of the USAF's night capability. During the brief air war the performance of the FLIR and lasers became legendary, as Pave Tack's 'chilling precision' (sic) became apparent. In one aircraft raid during the great 'tank plinking' operations against the 52nd Iraqi Armoured Brigade in early February, twenty F-111Fs dropped eighty GBU-12D/B LGBs, and with judicious 'squirts' from the Pave Tack laser gun successfully knocked out no fewer than 77 tanks in one fell swoop! Lt. Col. Tommy Crawford noted that FLIR was able to pick out dug-in targets in a manner that no other sensor could: 'We noticed that the bulldozer scrapes left a distinctive infra-red signature. The subsurface soil was a different make up of dirt; it absorbed heat and cooled off at a different rate than the surrounding sand'. Pave Tack's performance did not go unnoticed for long, according to another officer. 'When it was discovered that the F-111Fs had destroyed ten times more tanks than the F-16s, the [latter] were directed to cease attacks by mid-afternoon each day to allow the dust to settle before the "Varks" went to work at night! The F-111F was the "improved tactics" military briefers very coyly avoided talking about!'.

Mature by the time hostilities broke out in the Arabian Peninsula, for several years Pave Tack had been the precursor for the develop-

ment of a whole range of follow-on, more compact laser/FLIR targeting and navigation devices which entered the fray hot off the production lines, including the British TIALD (Thermal Imaging and Laser Designator) and the American LANTIRN (Low Altitude Navigation, Targeting Infra-Red for Night), both of which are now enjoying series production. These work on similar principles to those of Pave Tack and TRAM but make use of the latest microelectronics to reduce further the workload of the overtaxed air crews by means of enhanced resolution and automatic target-tracking.

The GEC-Marconi TIALD was ordered in June 1988 to meet Air Staff Requirement 1015, which mandated the establishment of a 'Pathfinder' squadron of all-weather laser bombers. Just over two years later, RAF Honington's Tornado recce-strike unit, No.

◄ F-4E Phantoms from the 3rd TFS *Peugeots* were assigned to the 7440th Combat Wing at Incirlik during the Gulf War. They were one of the last USAF Phantom strike units to use Pave Tack, though South Korean Phantoms retain the capability. (Frank B. Mormillo)

▶ Two TIALD pods were ferried to Tabuk in Saudi Arabia just in time for 'Desert Storm' action. The pods carried vulgar *Viz* comic-related artwork, which did not, however, detract from pod or air crew performance: the five Tornado GR.1s compatible with TIALD flew 95 laser combat sorties. (Bill Brookes Squadron Supplies)

◀ A-7E 'SLUFs' adopted bolt-on TI AN/AAR-49 FLIR pods tied in to the pilot's heads-up display for night and low-level nav and attack. These two aircraft, from VA-146 *Blue Diamonds*, were assigned to the USS *Constellation* when this photograph was taken, back in the halcyon days when Navy aircraft wore colourful, glossy paint schemes. The system was also packaged into select USAF A-7D/Ks as LANA (Low Altitude Night Attack). With the A-7 community fading out, the pods are being transferred to the OA-10A 'Wart Controller' establishment for night-time forward air control duties. (LTV)

13 Squadron, was earmarked for the task and worked up with the new 463lb pods under the direction of Sqn. Ldr. Greg Monaghan at RAF Boscombe Down before being declared combat-ready on 6 February 1991. Five machines in all were rewired for the system and they shared the two available pods, which carried the curious artwork 'Sandra' and 'Tracy' (based on the *Viz* 'Fat Slags' adult comic strip). The aircraft, flown by a mixture of crews drawn from RAF strike command, clocked up a total of 72 successful bombing missions between 10 and 27 February, opening up with attacks on the giant H3 Iraqi airfield in the south-west of the country with autonomous and 'buddy' designation for trios of CP-123/B 1,000lb LGBs and graduating with precision-guided deliveries against Al Asad and Habbinayah. TIALD represented a massive improvement

▶ 'Sparkle' mission symbols on 'Donna Ewin', a Tabuk-based Tornado GR.1, reflect the twenty lasing missions flown. The aircraft were capable of autonomous bombing and demonstrated this during strikes against Iraqi airfields; however, most of the missions were of the 'buddy' variety in support of the Red Sea-based Tornados, and extra 330 Imp. gallon fuel tanks were usually carried to extend their endurance. (Bill Brookes Squadron Supplies)

on the Buccaneer's Pave Spike 'gun', extending operations to night time and introducing an automatic lock-on facility unavailable to all but the IRADS-equipped F-117A Stealth bombers.[8]

LANTIRN has been in gestation longer. Built by Martin Marietta, this is a twinned arrangement which includes the AN/AAQ-13 TFR/FLIR navigation and -14 Laser/FLIR targeting pods, mounted under the inlet lips of the USAF's newest 'Teenagers', the F-16C 'Electric Jet', and F-15E 'Dual Role Fighter' (popularly known as the Strike Eagle, and also as the 'Mud Hen'). Like TIALD, the system had barely completed exhaustive development trials before being rushed to the war zone. F-15Es of the 335th TFS *Chiefs* deployed in December 1990 from Seymour-Johnson AFB, North Carolina, to Al Kharj in Saudi Arabia, just three months after achieving IOC with the system, and pooled its limited quantity of targeting pods with its sister squadron the 336th *Rocketeers*, which had been on station since the previous summer. Like TIALD, it acquitted itself well in combat, gaining fame for its Scud-busting exploits—although many attributed the success of the strikes not to LANTIRN but to the 'Mud Hen's' superb AN/APG-70 synthetic aperture radar (the imagery from which has to be seen to be believed) and to the preparatory Scud-hunting sorties flown by RAF recce Tornados. Its E-O systems have not yet reached the 'maturity' of the finely tuned Pave Tack, but operational develop-

ment is continuing apace and production is scheduled to embrace 561 of the nav systems and 441 of the targeting pods, with exports in prospect. The impending replacement of eighty *Liberty Wing* F-111Fs at their fifteen-year-old roost in Suffolk, England, by four dozen LANTIRN F-15Es will doubtless act as showcase for the technology. Another of the system's less publicized features is its terrain-mapping radar, which can be fused with the fighter's heads-up display to provide terrain clearance indicators combined with projected FLIR images of what lies ahead, for low-level work. These pods are more 'draggy' than the Pave Tack system they are replacing, but they do possess the supreme advantage that a 'down pod' does not necessarily mean a 'scrubbed' mission, as would be the case with an A-6E or F-111 with a 'SNAFU' terrain-following radar package: the pods can be downloaded and replaced in under twenty minutes, whereas fixes to the Intruder's or 'Aardvark's' radars has customarily required several hours' attention.

SUPERSMART

The Achilles' heel of all the infra-red systems is their poor performance in moist conditions, principally heavy cloud or fog. Like the sharply focused eyes of a sober fighter pilot, they can see through the night and cut through severe haze, but performance is sorry when their 'heads' are 'under the weather'! They are also exotic, must be manufactured under clinical conditions (and

▲ The Martin Marietta LANTIRN, composed of an AN/AAQ-13 navigation pod (port) and an AN/AAQ-14 targeting pod (starboard), has introduced a night, all-weather precision attack capability to the F-16. Also carried on the inlet lips of the USAF's F-15E 'Mud Hens', the system was used in combat by the Eagles of the *Fourth but First* operating out of Al Kharj, Saudi Arabia. (Martin Marietta)

▶ Schematics of the Martin Marietta LANTIRN (Low Altitude Navigation, Targeting Infra-Red for Night) dual-pod package used by F-15Es and F-16Cs. (USAF)

► The US Navy's answer to LANTIRN: the Ford Aerospace AN/AAS-38 FLIR pod and related AN/ASQ-173 laser spot tracker/strike camera (LST-SCAM), in service with the Fleet's F/A-18C Hornets. JP5 kerosene, a pair of AIM-9M Sidewinders and a quartet of Mk. 83 LDGP bombs make up the balance of the ironmongery strapped under this Marine Corps aircraft. (McAir)

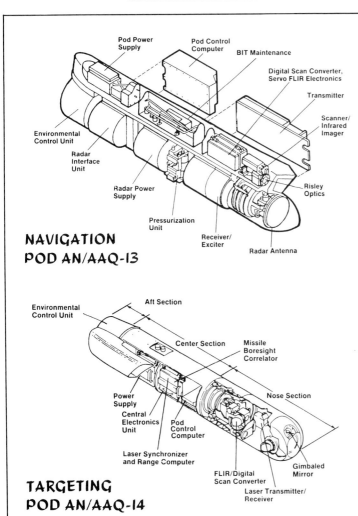

NAVIGATION POD AN/AAQ-13

Pod Power Supply
Pod Control Computer
BIT Maintenance
Digital Scan Converter, Servo FLIR Electronics
Transmitter
Scanner/Infrared Imager
Environmental Control Unit
Radar Interface Unit
Radar Power Supply
Pressurization Unit
Risley Optics
Receiver/Exciter
Radar Antenna

TARGETING POD AN/AAQ-14

Environmental Control Unit
Aft Section
Center Section
Missile Boresight Correlator
Nose Section
Power Supply
Central Electronics Unit
Pod Control Computer
Laser Synchronizer and Range Computer
FLIR/Digital Scan Converter
Laser Transmitter/Receiver
Gimbaled Mirror

maintained in a similar fashion in the field) and, apart from those employed internally, such as the Stealth fighter's flush kit, tend to have a deleterious effect on the user aircraft's endurance and signature—of ever increasing importance as 'strap-ons' steadily become less fashionable. The obvious answer is to embed the systems into the airframe, as has been done in the 'Bat Plane', but this is expensive and makes a meal out of simple maintenance tasks.[8] Another limitation of these E-O targeting systems is the inability to drop large quantities of weapons loads accurately in one big clout; instead, each 'smart' bomb or missile must be individually guided or locked on to its target. To address this shortfall, newer technologies are making their mark, some of which are rekindling the ancient arts—navigation and weapons delivery by the stars!

One of the most significant technologies to emerge since the perfection of FLIR is the Global Positioning System (GPS), or Navstar. Inaugurated in the mid-1970s in a fierce head-to-head competition between Magnavox and the ultimate victor, Rockwell-Collins, Navstar relies on a 'constellation' of transmitters placed in geosynchronous orbit to furnish precise three-dimensional co-ordinates. It leaps beyond the pitfalls of earlier 'radio' aids such as Omega and Loran to provide military aircraft equipped with the ARN-151(V) GPS receiver with exact position, velocity and time, altitude (mean sea level or absolute), steering information and waypoint

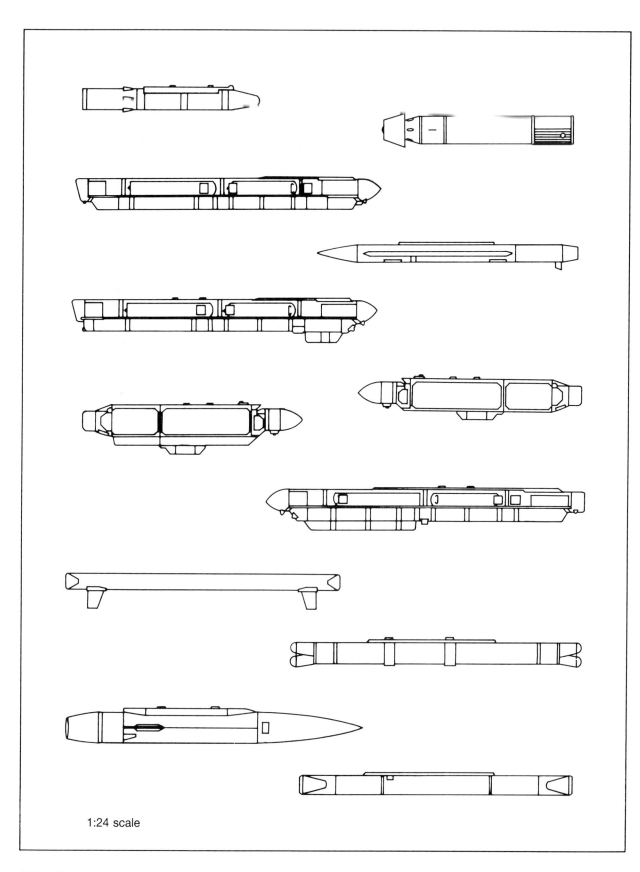

1:24 scale

data—including elevation from, and time and distance to, each planned navigation point. The system provides updates every second (with accuracy displayed as an alphanumeric 'figure of merit' at the top of the display panel) which, when fused with a back-up INS, FLIR 'eye', ballistics computer and projected film or electronic based moving map, permits all-weather, day or night precision attack. It is the keystone to the F-117A WSIP (Weapons Systems Improvement Program) and F-111F Project 'Pacer Strike' updates. What is perhaps most significant is that cheaper, simpler derivatives of this technology, together with TRN systems that have long since been applied to strategic nuclear weapons, are trickling into the world of conventional munitions.[9]

The earliest real attempt at guiding weapons by surreptitious means from afar originates in March 1972, when IBM and Lockheed were contracted to develop passive TDOA/DOA (time difference/direction of arrival) technology to triangulate the positions of 'enemy' radar sites, using a combination of atomic clocks at fixed ground sites together with newly developed elint receivers carried by trios of high-wheeling U-2C 'Dragon Ladies'. The processed target data was then intended to be relayed to defence-suppression missiles equipped with DME (Distance Measuring Equipment) receivers, such as the AGM-88 HARM and GBU-15 glide bomb, to fly them to, or point them precisely at, their targets. Development progressed through several phases and fiscal ups-and-downs, and cost and complexity escalated to the point where Congress and its General Accounting Office no longer felt able to support the effort.[10] It was eventually abandoned in FY 88 when nobody could find the $50 million needed for a European demonstration effort. In many respects, the system was simply far too specialized.

The introduction of extremely accurate miniaturized inertial reference sets and Navstar has rekindled this approach, but with infinitely broader applications, as a spin-off from the USAF Project 'Quick Drop' and US Navy IGTD (Inertially Guided Technology Demonstration).[11] Ordinary 'iron' bombs fitted with the new systems and modified steering vanes, now known as Joint Direct Attack Munitions, will be programmed with target co-ordinates and then let loose, in quantity if necessary from the cavernous hold of a B-52

or B-2. Using the hybrid navigation techniques, the bombs will then 'fly' themselves to the desired aimpoint before switching on their autonomous guidance for the terminal phase of flight, based on cheap seekers programmed with the infra-red, MMW radar or TV signatures of the specific targets. Bombers, in turn, can acquire this target data—embracing both fixed emitters and armoured columns—out of line of sight to the enemy defences by means of secure data-link terminals such as JTIDS (Joint Tactical Information Distribution System). These will decode and display the multitude of constantly updated 'near real-time' threat and target information and imagery down-linked by the great all-seeing 'eyes' flying backstage support: the Boeing E-3B AWACS plotting friendly and enemy aircraft; the Lockheed TR-1 radar-plotters; the Grumman E-8A JSTARS (Joint Surveillance Target Attack Radar System), tracking armour, truck convoys and trains with a SAR; and the soon-to-be-fielded ATARS (Advanced Tactical Aircraft Recon System, intended to equip Teledyne Ryan Model 234 Unmanned Air Vehicles), which will relay 'real time' FLIR and TV images of targets of special interest. The JDAMs will offer 10ft CEPs even when dropped in quantity at freefall stand-off ranges of up to 5–6 miles. 'Minimum engagement' will become a byword of attack crews.

FIGHTING WITH ELECTRONS

Despite the emerging stand-off weapons, there still exists the need to cope with the unexpected, be it a fighter or a sneaky triple-A battery. Anti-aircraft defences are becoming ever more portable and reliable—and are relying all the more on sophisticated E-O acquisition and terminal guidance technology, to which the SEAD forces are presently 'blind'. Countering these threats is accomplished in a predominantly automatic manner by 'switch on and leave' integrated electronic warfare suites which combine passive radar and laser receivers with active emitters, and disposables such as chaff, flares and active decoys. From these have emerged a host of 'strap-ons' and metalline or glass excrescences which intermingle with the clutches of bombs, missiles and designators carried by front-line military aircraft.

RF-spectrum jamming pods came to the fore during the Vietnam War, where Quick

Reaction Contracts (QRCs) were issued to General Electric and Hughes for the rapid development of systems capable of 'whiting out' radars and swamping automatic gain receivers with noise. Aircraft flying in set formations and jamming in a combined 'Beacon' mode could, between them, deny the enemy accurate azimuth and range data, making them relatively impervious to the ravages of the infamous SA-2 'Guideline' and radar-directed AAA. Similar devices abounded to fool the conical-scan 'Spin Can' dishes of the MiGs, while rearguard broadband jamming aircraft like the EA-6A Intruder and EB-66 Destroyer 'whited out' the low-frequency early warning, ranging and height-finding devices which carried the imaginative NATO codenames 'Flat Face', 'Spoonrest', 'Squat Eye' and 'Thin Skin'. By 1972 and the inauguration of 'Linebacker', Westinghouse had entered the fray with its AN/ALQ-101 jammer, which was subsequently revisited and enlarged, with the addition of a new 'gondola', to create the AN/ALQ-119. This introduced fine-tuned noise and deception jamming by means of advanced solid state TWT (travelling wave tube) electronics which kept pace with the frequency-hopping antics of the anti-aircraft radars and introduced such novel techniques as the 'Transponder Mode' or 'range gate stealing' (to generate spurious range data by means of delayed action copycat pulses), and the 'Repeater Mode' (using amplitude modulation out of phase with the threat to generate false azimuth), so that the enemy defences

pumped SAMs and triple-A harmlessly into 'ghosts', some distance away from their intended victims.

The introduction in the Sinai in the autumn of 1973 of the Soviet-designed 'Straight Flush' continuous wave (CW) illuminating radar and its allied, portable SA-6 'Gainful' SAMs (which work in the same fashion as SARH in the AAM world) prompted yet more sophisticated technology, from which emerged the first truly integrated tactical EW systems, capable of acting without the detailed intervention of a specialized electronic warfare officer. The USAF 'Compass Matrix/Tie' package, for example, mated Applied Technology's broad-spectrum radar warning receivers (listening in the 0.5–18gc range) with the Westinghouse AN/ALQ-119, so that output was apportioned to the threats—a technique known as 'power management'—and after 1979 with its follow-on modular AN/ALQ-131, capable of handling forty different waveforms, including the new CW illuminators, simultaneously.[12] It has been a virtually endless catalogue of updates, with the US Navy treading its own path with a series of Sanders-built deception-jamming devices such as the AN/ALQ-100, -126 and newer ITT -165 ASPJ (Advanced Self-Programming Jammer) which equip most of the Fleet.

Now far more aware of the harsh realities of today's fierce anti-aircraft environment, made even more problematic following the emergence of the Russian and Ukrainian hardware-for-hard-currency policy of offer-

▼ The war in South-East Asia proved to be the spur for the development of a whole line of RF-spectrum electronic countermeasures pods, including the 'long', multiple-band Westinghouse AN/ALQ-101(V) noise jammer, developed under QRC-335. The pod was later modified with a gondola and still serves with the RAF's front-line Jaguar and Buccaneer units in the modernized 'Vee-10' configuration. (Westinghouse)

▲ A Northrop AN/ALQ-171 ECM pod is wheeled into place on Lt. Col. Roger Taylor's TAWC-based F-16A. This pod was developed for export but is used in limited numbers for air defence training, simulating 'enemy' countermeasures. (Northrop)

▶ The Qatar Emirates flew its Mirage F1s on joint operations with the American 614th TFS *Lucky Devils*, out of Doha, Qatar. This desert and sky blue Mirage, here receiving an official send off, totes an outboard DB 3163 Remora ECM pod. (TSgt. F. Lee Corkran/USAF)

◄ The Westinghouse AN/ALQ-101 was enlarged to create the -119, which introduced 'power management' as well as deception-jamming techniques. This 'short', two-band model was used by F-111E/Fs and A-7D/Ks. (Robin A. Walker via Peter E. Davies)

◄ The 'long' AN/ALQ-119(V), in common with its contemporaries, originally wore a white and black scheme. This gave way to olive green during the mid-1980s, and the finish has since been changed again, to medium compass grey. (Westinghouse)

ing their latest SAM and radar technology at knock-down prices, Western European countries have stirred from their slumber and have created jamming pods of indigenous design—the convincingly effective Sky Shadow, Barex, TMV 015 Barem and DB 3163 Remora bolted to Jaguars, Mirages and Tornados—or have taken up options on the Westinghouse, Sanders and Loral hardware.

The latest in the American series, such as the Raytheon-modified AN/ALQ-184(V)-1 which entered service with the 'Wild Weasel' community in February 1987 on a trials basis, have introduced such technology as a pair of Rotman Lenses. These each feature an electronic 'daisy' array of eight elements which can focus energy precisely in the direction of the threat radars, to increase ERP (effective radiated power) tenfold.[13] At the height of the air war in the Persian Gulf, only 25 per cent of the American land-based combat aircraft could be mustered for attack duties at any one time because there were not enough of these various pods to go around. One Penta-gon official likened the highly prized aids to an American Express credit card, inasmuch as pilots 'wouldn't leave home without one!'. This prudence paid off: only three of their aircraft losses were attributed to Iraqi radar-guided missiles. Three hundred obsolescent Westinghouse AN/ALQ-101 and -119 pods were used to supplement the 130 Block 1 (manual intervention), 260 Block 2 ('hands off') AN/ALQ-131 and forty AN/ALQ-184 jam-mers available to USAF theatre commanders. Orders are pending for 590 AN/ALQ-184s, with options for up to 400 more, while updates for less conspicuous devices carried internally by F-15Es, F-111Fs and EF-111A blanket-jammers continues. That they worked so well over war-torn Kuwait and Iraq is testimony enough to the technology: dur-ing the prewar 'Desert Shield' build-up, sceptical mission-planners were talking with some candour of losing one hundred aircraft a week. Thankfully, their worst fears soon dissipated.

Accompanying the jamming pods amidst

the plethora of 'stores' are the diverse chaff/flare/decoy dispensers, packaged as pods or sprouting from pylons and fuselages as prominent blisters. Again, the USAF has been the most prodigious developer in this field ever since the RAF came up with the idea back in the Second World War, when Halifaxes of No. 100 Group, the countermeasures force, dropped bundles of 'Window'—aluminium foil strips cut to suitable dipole lengths to create thousands of spurious radar returns. During the postwar years Britain applied her vast EW 'institutional knowledge' exclusively to her V-bombers, while the rest of Europe chose to do nothing and tac-air became increasingly reliant on speed alone as a means of survival.

To a certain degree, the United States adopted a similar posture—until the Vietnam War, when tactical strike jets undertook aerial offensives of a strategic nature and very quickly needed all the protection they could muster. The QRCs which had given birth to the small white pods with their multiplex of aerials were accompanied by developments which introduced a series of dispensers ranging from the simple, such as tinsel-like chaff ('Window'), to the sophisticated, like cesium lamps which put out 'puffs' of invisible infra-red energy to lure heat-seeking missiles away from their intended quarry.

▲ The Westinghouse AN/ALQ-131(V) modular jammer features both noise- and deception-jamming techniques and can cope with forty different waveforms. The shallow version seen attached to an A-10A 'Hog' in the first photograph is a two-band version, also commonly employed on F-111E/Fs. The version fitted to the Phantom is a three-band model, now widely used by the F-16. (Author)

▶ A Muharraq-based Jaguar taxies along the runway, post-strike, with an AN/ALQ-101(V)-10 under its wing. The pod proved to be surprisingly effective during Operation 'Desert Storm', despite its twenty-year-old design. The reciprocal starboard pylon was used for the Matra Phimat chaff dispenser. Flares were disgorged from a pair of AN/ALE-40s bolted under the rear fuselage. (Royal Air Force)

These countermeasures also were introduced to combat during the late 1960s in large pods, among them the MB Associates AN/ALE-2 and follow-on -38/41 bulk chaff dispensers which were capable of 'sowing' clouds of blanketing reflectors based on up to 360lb of tinsel or aluminized fibreglass strands, and the Northrop AN/AAQ-8 infra-red countermeasures pod, fifty of which were built for use by barrage-jammer EB-66C/E Destroyers and the MC/130E 'Combat Talons' of the Special Operations Squadrons (which use the devices to this day, suspended precariously under their wing tanks). These have been joined by new pods such as the Loral AN/ALQ-123, equipping US Navy jets, and a range of 'disco light' devices which are fitted to Western attack helicopters.

More widespread self-defence packages designed to fox the terminal threats away from their targets during the closing stages of the deadly encounter with SAMs and AAMs flourished immediately following the Yom Kippur conflict, the catalyst for so many developments. Most have been supplied by Tracor Industries as common modules which can be readily adapted to a number of aircraft. The US Navy AN/ALE-39 'round holer' equips all that Service's aircraft and those of its foreign customers, while the USAF AN/ALE-40 'square shooter', fielded originally on Israeli F-4E Phantoms in 1974, has been adapted to just about every NATO

◀ Sixty-seven Tornado GR.1/1As were resprayed in the 'Pink Panther' scheme for desert duties and 61 of them saw action in the Gulf. This example demonstrates the high-speed, low-level flying techniques employed early in the war, though here in the peaceful skies above Fairford. The outboard pod is a high-capacity BOZ-107 chaff/flare dispenser, used in lieu of the AN/ALE-40 'Square Shooters' installed in the F.3 air defence versions. (Author)

◀ Keeping cool under cover, a Tornado GR.1 shows off its BOZ-107 dispenser to the camera. (Royal Air Force)

► Tracor-MB Associates of San Ramon, California, developed this high-capacity AN/ALE-38 chaff dispenser for the purpose of 'sowing' corridors with the radar-blanking material. For a short while the mission was assigned to the AQM-34V unmanned air vehicle, deployed and controlled remotely by DC-130A/E 'Combat Angel' motherships. ALE-38s remain on the inventory and have been used to provide countermeasures 'clutter' during air-to-air tests of the AMRAAM missile. (USAF)

machine with the self-respect to label itself a 'front-line aircraft'—the haste with which these were retrofitted to RAF Tornados during the Operation 'Granby' build-up was commendable. Both systems are now being supplanted by the AN/ALE-47, retaining the two classical formats of round and rectangular expendables but packaged with the latest in chaff, fierce-burning infra-red flare decoys and active RF-spectrum emitters which are capable of emulating the signals discharged by threat emitters. RF-spectrum emitters are a radical new category, introduced in the mid-1980s as the Sanders Poet (Primed Oscillator Expendable Transponder), and have evolved into the TI Genex (Generation-X). Bulk dispensers remain in use, as exemplified by the Tornado's multiple-capacity BOZ-107 pods and the Mirage's

Sycomor, which remain useful for a number of special assignments, including pathfinding missions. Towed expendables and larger, more sophisticated Mk. 82 bomb-sized decoys such as the Brunswick Samson and ADM-141A TALD (Tactical Air-Launched Decoy) are also to be seen in increasing numbers festooning the stores pylons of Western attack and support aircraft.[14] Development is also rapid in the fields of combined Missile Approach Warning System (MAWS) technology, using Doppler radar, and of cryogenic receivers working supersensitively at around 77°K (−196°C) along with laser receiver/interrogators, designed to compensate for the existing EO 'blindspot'. These will activate chaff, flares and Gen-X active decoys at precisely the right moment, and in the right combination, to foil the 'smarter'

► Loral built the AN/ALQ-123 infra-red countermeasures pod for the US Navy. One of the first IR deception jammers to be fielded, it emits 'puffs' of distracting energy to lure heat-seeking missiles away from the aircraft. Here the pod is strapped to the port outboard station of a Naval Air Reserve A-7B of VA-305 *Lobos*. (Loral)

SAMs and AAMs. American EW specialists Lockheed-Sanders, Loral and Cincinatti Electronics lead the field, with Britain, France and Sweden also involved in this work. Such integrated packages should be the norm by the time the Lockheed F-22 Advanced Tactical Fighter, Dassault-Breguet Rafale, EFA (European Fighter Aircraft) and Saab Gripen reach operational maturity at the start of the new millenium.

The complexities involved in how all this technology intertwines to provide a high degree of confidence in both weapons-on-target and air crew survival will doubtless occupy the minds of aviation historians for decades to come, as old wars are re-examined in the light of freshly declassified papers and newer devices are committed to combat.

NOTES TO CHAPTER FIVE

1. The first laser was built in 1960 by the US physicist Theodore Maiman, who realized earlier theoretical work dating back to Einstein. Refer to the Glossary for a fuller explanation.

2. See Chapter 2 for further details of the Paveway I bombs' combat exploits.

3. Basic TV and light-amplified LLLTV work with visible light in the same manner as closed-circuit TV and video cameras. FLIR works by picking up invisible infra-red energy. Refer to the Glossary for a fuller explanation.

4. Refer to Chapter 2. Buccaneer tactics were typical of early USAF Pave Knife and Pave Spike techniques, which used either autonomous bombing or high-altitude or 'pop-up' 'buddy' lasing.

5. A reversal of the philosophy behind the US Navy TRIM package, which witnessed the use of elecro-optic sensors purely as a supplement to radar target-tracking for 'Commando Hunt' operations. A-6E TRAM and F-111F Pave Tack crews 'follow the [radar] bar' as range to target closes in, then divert attention to FLIR as the primary targeting system—though Capt. Mike Conway pointed out to the author some time prior to 'Desert Storm' that 'You would get involved over your target without radar'. Relying mainly on FLIR, which is a passive device, also has stealth benefits. New aircraft like the LANTIRN F-15E, which can speedily produce a SAR radar 'patch' or 'strip' map and then 'freeze' it, with only periodic updates thereafter, can use FLIR in this manner to great advantage.

6. Following the recent demise of the A-12 Avenger II stealth bomber, the trusty Grumman product will remain at the forefront of naval aviation for at least another decade, rewinged and 'SWIPed' (System Weapons Improvement Programmed) to return their fatigue clocks back to zero. A total of 294 aircraft are receiving the new wings.

7. The 4th TFW at Seymour-Johnson AFB, North Carolina, was the first Phantom unit to achieve IOC with the system in April 1983. It relinquished the mission during 1989 when the unit began conversion to F-15Es. The 3rd TFS *Peugeots*, equipped with Pave Tack F-4Es until 1991 at Clark Field in the Philippines, deployed six Phantoms to Incirlik, Turkey, for Gulf War operations, but their pods arrived too late for combat. Other reports suggest that these aircraft were fitted with Pave Spike instead, but the different training requirements for the pods precluded their use in combat.

8. IRADS is cued by a computer-modelled digital flight-plan, kept on track by an exotic Honeywell INS known as the SPN/GEANS based on an electrostatically suspended beryllium gyro. This system, due to be replaced by a Honeywell Ring-Laser Gyro and Rockwell Navstar, helps keep the pair of infra-red systems—one forward-looking and the other downward-looking and hence known as the DLIR—on target by constantly computing aircraft-versus-target position and assists the pilots in tracking their crosshaired quarry with accuracies measured to within one metre. TIALD, when interfaced with the Tornado's nav-and-attack gear, introduced commensurate auto-tracking technology 'in a can'.

9. See Chapter 4 for an explanation of Terrain-Reference Navigation technology.

10. It began as a spin-off from the Project 'Pave Onyx', called the ALSS (Advanced Location Strike System) and subsequently referred to as the PELSS (Precision Emitter Location Strike System), then PLSS (Precision Location Strike System) and ultimately SLATS (Signal Location and Targeting System). In 1972, during tests at White Sands missile range, New Mexico, the U-2C/ALSS helped guide four DME-assisted GBU-8 Hobos to an average of 75ft from the target dishes. The TR-1A/PLSS was exercised at a 'Green Flag' manoeuvre at Nellis AFB, Nevada, during April 1987 and the relevant hardware remains, inactive, at Beale AFB, California. The TR-1A-equipped 95th RS 'Ass Kickers' stationed at RAF Alconbury in England are capable of plotting target positions in 'near real-time' by means of ASARS-2 and 'Senior Spear Phase IV' SLIR and sigint sensors, 'netted' into NATO's intelligence system.

11. Both Boeing and Northrop were contracted to produce IGTD trials rounds during 1987. Captive test flights at Edwards and China Lake, California, led to Phase Two drops at Eglin, Florida, beginning the following July. The basic inertial/GPS system provides CEPs of 'tens of feet'; when a pre-programmed JDAM seeker is fitted as well, accuracy mirrors that of today's best 'smart' bombs. Intended user aircraft will include the B-2A, which will be capable of dropping up to 76 inertial/GPS 500lb bombs simultaneously.

12. The AN/ALQ-131 can be programmed on the flight-line with a suitable 'jamming strategy' in less than half an hour; by contrast, it took up to eight hours to reconfigure the AN/ALQ-119 as the pod had to be physically disassembled and adjusted in the electronics shop.

13. Radar effectiveness decreases by the fourth power in relation to range, making target acquisition a tense and difficult process; aircraft, too, are subject to the same laws of diminishing returns but are in theory capable of drawing on the massive electrical output created by their gas turbine engne generators (miniature versions of those used in hydro-electric power stations!). By tuning their jamming to the same frequencies as the threats ('power management'), and pointing the energy at them (via antenna steering or a Rotmen Lens), the little pods are capable of overwhelming large radars possessing comparatively huge apertures. By the same token, it is the large radar, combined with the enormous power available, which renders AWACS and its Soviet counterpart the SUWACs so incredibly effective.

14. Credit must also go to the dedicated EW craft which ply their trade with electrons at some distance behind the scenes, to keep the enemy radar air defence networks confused and their communications systems all but useless: the F-4G 'Wild Weasels' and their European equivalents the Tornado ECRs; the EF-111A Raven and EA-6B Prowler; and the venerable EC-130H 'Compass Call'. As 'Wild Weasel Guru' and head of USAF's prestigious Tactical Air Warfare Center, Gen. John Corder pointed out to the technical press at a briefing a short while after the conclusion of Operation 'Desert Storm', at least two MiG 'kills' should have been shared with the EW folk. Apparently, the Iraqi pilots didn't know what was going on because 'Compass Call' interfered with their communications radios!

GLOSSARY

-/A Suffix used to denote a 'strap-on' which remains attached to the aircraft, e.g. the SUU-23/A Vulcan pod.

AAA Anti-aircraft artillery. Also known as 'triple-A'.

AAM Air-to-air missile. Also known as air intercept missile.

AAQ Airborne infra-red, special type, targeting system, e.g. the AAQ-14 LANTIRN targeting pod.

ADM Air-launched decoy or drone missile.

AGL Above ground level (in feet).

AGM air-to-ground missile. The American term for ASM.

AIM Air intercept missile. The American term for AAM.

AIR Air Inflatable Retard. A parachute-cum-balloon ('Ballute') version of the Vietnam-era Mk. 82 Snakeye, also available in larger yields.

ALE Airborne countermeasures, ejection. A chaff, flare and active decoy dispenser.

ALQ Airborne countermeasures, special-purpose pod or installation.

ARM Anti-radiation missile, e.g., the air-launched ALARM.

ASM Air-to-surface missile.

ATKRON US Navy Attack Squadron.

ATLIS French Automatic Tracking Laser Illumination System, similar to the British TIALD and American AAQ-, AVQ- and ASQ- optical targeting systems.

AVQ Airborne-visual, special type, e.g. the AN/AVQ-26 Pave Tack infra-red and laser targeting pod.

AVTR Airborne video tape recorder.

AWACS Airborne Warning and Control System, usually associated with today's Boeing E-3 Sentry but introduced to combat thirty years ago by Lockheed's EC-121 'Big Eye'.

AWW Airborne armament remote control, e.g. the AN/AWW-9 data-link. See below.

AXQ Airborne television, special type, e.g. the AN/AXQ-14 TV data-link pod. Similar to the AWW.

-/B Suffix used to denote a 'strap-on' which is released from an aircraft, e.g. the BLU-109/B penetrating bomb.

B/N See WSO.

BAe British Aerospace plc.

BDU Bomb, Dummy Unit. A training bomb, e.g. the BDU-33.

BLU Bomb, Live Unit (pronounced 'Bloo'). The generic NATO term for any live explosive unit, whether an entire system, such as the BLU-107 Durandal, or a component of a store, such as the BLU-97 CEM bomblet.

BRU Bomb Release Unit. The bomb racks employed by F-111s and other newer generation aircraft such as the F-15E; cf. MER/TER.

BVR Beyond visual range.

-/C Release mechanism retained within the weapons bay, e.g. the MAU-12/C racks fitted to the bomb bay of the F-111E.

'Canned' Any attack manoeuvre which has clearly defined parameters of airspeed, altitude and/or dive angle and weapons release height AGL. The term is also used

to denote strictly defined flight plans, including climb and descent procedures.

CAP Combat Air Patrol, also known as MiGCAP, BARCAP (carrier zone barrier) and TARCAP (target area) patrols.

CBU Cluster Bomb Unit, e.g. the CBU-89 Gator. These weapons are time-delayed or proximity-fused to split in two at a preset height above ground level, releasing up to 700 submunitions (depending on the model's contents). CBUs may also be used to dispense FAE canisters and, in limited circumstances, propaganda leaflets.

CCIP Continuously Computed Impact Point. The modern term for computer-assisted visual bombing. See also CEP.

CEM Combined Effects (sub)Munitions capable of destroying either 'soft' or semi-'hard' targets by means of hybrid fragmentation/incendiary and hollow-shaped charges, packed into the SUU-65 canister to form the CBU-87.

CEP Circular Error Probable, or bomb miss distance from the chosen impact point (also known as CEA or Circular Error Average, especially with nuclear weapons). CEPs are usually measured angularly in 'mils' accuracy, a function of aircraft slant-range to target and the accuracy of the aircraft's on-board systems. In effect, one mil equates to a one-foot CEP at one thousand feet, so that, for example, an A-7E Corsair II with 12 mils of bombing accuracy in the CCIP mode which released 'dumb' bombs from 10,000ft would expect to deposit its ordnance within an average of 120ft from the target. CEPs tend to degrade further at altitude because of the difficulty in acquiring targets visually.

CPU Prefix for British laser-guided munitions; cf. American KMU- and GBU-designations.

CRV Canadian Rocket Vehicle, e.g. the high-velocity CRV-7.

E-O Electro-Optics, including TV and LLLTV.

-eye The suffix used to denote a weapon developed by the US Naval Weapons Center (formerly known as the Naval Ordnance Test Station) at China Lake, California, e.g. the Mk. 15 Snakeye fin used with the Mk. 82 and Mk. 36 DST, or the Mk. 20 Rockeye cluster bomb.

EWO Electronic Warfare Officer. A navigator (see WSO) who is skilled at electronic warfare techniques as well as 'weaponeering'.

FAE Fuel-air explosive. Originally known as Explosive Fuel Munitions (EFMs), these weapons mix fuel with the surrounding air and then ignite the resulting vapour, creating tremendous atmospheric overpressures.

FFAR Folding-Fin Aerial Rocket, tube launched from an LAU or SUU dispenser.

FLIR Forward-looking infra-red. All bodies at temperatures above absolute zero radiate electromagnetic energy, ranging in wavelength from short cosmic rays, through gamma rays, X-rays, the ultraviolet, visible radiation, infra-red and so on. With FLIR, energy from the infra-red part of the spectrum is collected and a thermal image generated by rearranging the signal from the detector to form a spatial analogue of the original scene. The degree of infra-red emission from any body is subject to its properties as a 'heat' radiator and thus the image is a 'false' one to the human eye. Darker objects tend to absorb heat more quickly by day and subsequently radiate heat more quickly by night. Heat 'generators', such as people and engines, show up well at all times. The resulting scene may be displayed in either the 'white hot' mode (which closely resembles a black and white negative) or as a 'black hot' image (a positive image).

FMS Foreign military sales, authorized by Congress and often handled with the US forces acting as an intermediary for the purposes of support.

FOV Field of view (of a weapon or targeting pod sensor or seeker). Virtually all TV and FLIR devices have several fixed 'zoom' settings, or a variable FOV.

GBU Guided Bomb Unit, e.g. the GBU-15.

GD General Dynamics Corporation.

HAS Hardened aircraft shelter.

IOC Initial Operating Capability. The first time a new aircraft or system becomes operational with a squadron-sized unit.

KMU American Vietnam-era designation for very early test GBUs (e.g. the KMU-342 750lb LGB), and for the original laser guidance kits or 'groups' once the term GBU was adopted.

Laser Light amplification by the stimulated emission of radiation—a cascade of coherent photons. Its key advantage is its ability to travel considerable distances undiminished in intensity, made possible by its coherent, non-spreading beam. This makes the laser ideally suited for ranging and target marking, and considerably more accurate than radar. The war in South-East Asia witnessed the introduction of the first practical chemical lasers in combat. They are not true 'Buck

◄ Squatting beneath a No. 56 Squadron *Firebirds* Phantom FGR.2 at RAF Wattisham, ground crewmen carefully manoeuvre an AIM-7E-2 Sparrow III into the aft port missile well. Sparrow remains the primary radar-guided armament on the RAF's dwindling force of 'Fox Fours', though Sky Flash also is used by the Port Stanley detachment. (Royal Air Force)

Rogers' ray guns, although work in that field is already well underway, with emphasis on self-defence against AAMs and SAMs.

LDGP Low drag, general-purpose bomb, e.g. the Mk. 82 'slick', or conical-finned bomb.

LGB Laser-guided bomb unit, e.g. the GBU-10.

LLLGB Low-level laser-guided bomb, e.g. the Paveway III GBU-24.

LLLTV Low-light-level TV sensor. An airborne E-O version of a 'Starlight' scope.

LOC Lines of communication. LOC targets are typically choke-points such as bridges, railway marshalling yards and motorway bottlenecks.

MER Multiple ejection rack, which expands pylon carriage capability from one store to six, though four is typical, in either 'Slant Four' configuration (lower and outwards-facing side attachment points, such as when on a wing), or 'Flat Four' (side attachment points only, such as on a ventral fuselage station).

NFO See WSO.

NOTS Naval Ordnance Test Station. Known as the NWC since 1967.

NWC Naval Weapons Center. The chief development centre for the US Navy's weapons systems, located at China Lake, California.

Pave- A prefix standing for Precision Avionics Vectoring Equipment, born during the Vietnam War to denote any system developed (usually) by the Eglin Munitions Systems Division (known, prior to 1990, as the Armament Development Test Center) aimed at enhancing strike accuracy, e.g. the AVQ-23 Pave Spike laser designator.

PGM Precision-guided munitions. The official term for so-called 'smart' bombs and missiles.

pK The assured probability of a 'kill', expressed as a percentage based on the numbers of weapons expended. An AIM-120 pK of 80 per cent means that four out of five of the missiles would destroy their targets.

POL Petroleum, oil and lubricants (storage facilities).

RAF Royal Air Force.

SAC Strategic Air Command, now being realigned under the new USAF Air Combat Command.

SAM Surface-to-air missile.

SRAM Short-Range (nuclear) Attack Missile, generally used to denote the AGM-69 but later used for the now cancelled second-generation SRAM-2 and -T models.

STARM The GD AGM-78 Standard Anti-Radiation Missile, known to the US Navy at STARM and to the USAF as the Standard ARM.

SUU Suspension Underwing Unit. An airborne dispenser, e.g. the SUU-21 practice pod or SUU-30 CBU casing.

TAC American Tactical Air Command, now being realigned under the new USAF Air Combat Command.

TER Triple ejection rack, which triples pylon carriage capability. Bombs and other stores weighing up to 1,000lb are carried in either threes, 'Slant Two' or 'Flat Two' configurations. See MER.

TI Texas Instruments Inc.

TIALD Thermal Imaging and Laser Designator pod, employed by Tornado GR.1 strike aircraft.

VFR Visual flight rules. Clear weather; daytime.

WESTPAC A West Pacific cruise, especially one made by a Carrier and Air Group (CAG) to the Tonkin Gulf during the Vietnam War.

WSO, 'Wizzo' Weapons Systems Officer. A USAF term to denote a navigator trained as a weapons specialist in two-seat fighter-bombers. Most other air arms refer to him as a navigator. The US Navy refers to its Naval Flight Officers (NFOs) either as Radar Intercept Officers (RIOs, e.g. the backseater in the F-14 Tomcat) or as Bombardier/Navigators (B/Ns, e.g. the right-hand seaters in the A-6 Intruder). The concept evolved during the latter half of the 1960s when fighters introduced complex navigation, electronic warfare and targeting systems.

INDEX